Code Musicology

CRITICAL PERSPECTIVES ON MUSIC AND SOCIETY

Series Editor
David Arditi, University of Texas at Arlington

This book series produces books that present a critical perspective on popular music and the music industry. Two dominant strains of thought exist for the study of popular music. First, many texts in the popular culture tradition celebrate the artists, fans, and cultures that arise from popular music. Second, Music Industry Studies texts give students a "how-to" perspective on making it in the music industry. In both cases, texts rarely address the way that the music industry produces and reproduces power. The purpose of this book series is to provide a platform for authors who explore the social production of music; as such it is broadly interdisciplinary.

The series invites submissions by scholars from the fields of cultural studies, American studies, history, sociology, literature, communication, media studies, music, women's studies, ethnic studies, popular culture, music industry studies, political science, economics, and history.

Specific topics addressed:

- Musicians as Labor
- Identity (Sex, Gender, Race, Ethnicity, Disability, and Sexuality)
- Critical Representations
- Music Industry Studies
- Music in the Global South
- Production of Genres
- New/Old Technologies
- Sound Studies
- Access inequalities to music production and consumption
- Spaces of music production, creation, and consumption

Code Musicology: From Hardwired to Software by Denis Crowdy
Mixtape Nostalgia: Culture, Memory, and Representation by Jehnie I. Burns
iTake-Over: The Recording Industry in the Streaming Era, Second Edition by David Arditi
Cruisicology: The Music Culture of Cruise Ships by David Cashman and Philip Hayward
"This Is America": Race, Gender, and Politics in America's Musical Landscape by Katie Rios

Code Musicology
From Hardwired to Software

Denis Crowdy

LEXINGTON BOOKS
Lanham • Boulder • New York • London

Published by Lexington Books
An imprint of The Rowman & Littlefield Publishing Group, Inc.
4501 Forbes Boulevard, Suite 200, Lanham, Maryland 20706
www.rowman.com

86-90 Paul Street, London EC2A 4NE

Copyright © 2022 by The Rowman & Littlefield Publishing Group, Inc.

All rights reserved. No part of this book may be reproduced in any form or by any electronic or mechanical means, including information storage and retrieval systems, without written permission from the publisher, except by a reviewer who may quote passages in a review.

British Library Cataloguing in Publication Information Available

Library of Congress Cataloging-in-Publication Data

Names: Crowdy, Denis, author.
Title: Code musicology : from hardwired to software / Denis Crowdy.
Description: Lanham : Lexington Books, 2022. | Series: Critical perspectives on music and society | Includes bibliographical references and index. | Summary: "Code Musicology opens a conduit between musicology and software studies. It extends an ethnomusicology of technoculture from the world of hardware and the hardwired to software, code, and algorithms and directs attention to IT industries and software-centered transnational commerce as a result of sectorial transformation"— Provided by publisher.
Identifiers: LCCN 2022016449 (print) | LCCN 2022016450 (ebook) | ISBN 9781666909197 (cloth) | ISBN 9781666909210 (paper) | ISBN 9781666909203 (ebook)
Subjects: LCSH: Music—Computer programs. | Music—Philosophy and aesthetics. | Music and technology.
Classification: LCC ML74 .C76 2022 (print) | LCC ML74 (ebook) | DDC 780.285/65—dc23
LC record available at https://lccn.loc.gov/2022016449
LC ebook record available at https://lccn.loc.gov/2022016450

Contents

Acknowledgments	vii
Introduction: The Rise of Code	1
1 The Life of Code	11
2 Life around Code	23
3 Coding Constraints	35
4 Coding Aesthetics	53
5 A Software Development Perspective	67
6 Code on the Move	87
Conclusion	101
Appendix 1: Definitions	117
Appendix 2: Twotrack App Reviews Discussed	119
References	123
Index	135
About the Author	141

Acknowledgments

Thanks to the following people for discussions, thoughts, comments on drafts at various stages: Andrew Alter, Steve Collins, Ian Collinson, Glenn Dickins, Peter Doyle, Heather Horst, Sarah Keith, Jay LeBoeuf, Alex Mesker, Pat O'Grady, Adrian Renzo, Leigh Smith, and Tim Taylor. A special thanks to Mary Mainsbridge and Nicole Matthews for their time, insights, and truly collegial support that really pushed the project along at critical moments. The book would not have been possible without the provision of extended periods of research leave and funds to allow travel by my Department at Macquarie University. The support provided by an Australian Research Council linkage grant, LP150100973, "Music, Mobile Phones and Community Justice in Melanesia" has supported vital elements of the research behind the book. Thanks to family members Rob Crowdy and Janet Crowdy for reading the manuscript. I am grateful for the enthusiasm Courtney Morales and David Arditi have shown in supporting the project and the manuscript has benefited greatly from changes made as a result of the anonymous review process. Finally, thanks as always to Gima, Mareta, and Patrick (and Nabjit) for their patience, perspective, and support throughout.

Introduction

The Rise of Code

Reveling in a newly untethered listening environment after buying some expensive Bluetooth headphones, I read an article where people were worried that such devices may have been invading their privacy. How, I thought, mentally tracing the audio signal? They are wireless, sure, but where would data about my listening practices leak? Only via an app, as it turns out, which I had installed. I checked the app store entry for the software, and it clearly states, "This app may use your location even when it isn't open, which can decrease device battery life." Having developed apps myself, and in the process made decisions as to what permissions to seek from users to carry out relevant functions, this seemed like over-reach. Actually I was less surprised about a potential breach of my privacy as I was about my naivety where an app had become involved. This is the age of big data, or big music as Koutsomichalis (2016) puts it, where data collection and surveillance are fundamental to the operation of music commerce under a stage of capitalism characterized by Arditi (2021) as "unending consumption" (23).

Earlier in the day I had been teaching university students principles of signal flow in our recording studio, encouraging everyone to follow the inputs, cables, and outputs. Following the wires to visualize signal flow helps identify problems and is essential for creativity and processing sound in the studio. It occurred to me, however, that for much of the day sitting at a computer, writing, coding, listening, there had been no visible wires. My previous headphones had been tethered to my computer, and that cable served as a reminder of the sort of signal flow that was part of how I thought about recorded music. Now, however, it was only at the very last moment situated right around my ears that the headphones themselves carried out a conversion from digital to analog, before the speaker in them transformed that signal into air pressure waves to be perceived as sound. What data movement via the app and the absence of a final headphone wire highlighted to me was the increasing ineffectiveness of a serial, wired abstraction in everyday musical contexts. A lot more is going on in a digital environment, and the paths can be very indirect. How effective is it to imagine a direct wired path from source to speaker in a world where data can be sent to third parties on the other side of the planet as a side-effect? On the train commute home I observed the ubiquity of Bluetooth headphones. Many of us were now routinely carrying code around on our heads.

For many years now, a great deal of everyday musical activity has occurred in a digital domain. So much of the signal path is now digital, in fact, that the term feels redundant. Certainly, I have colleagues who cringe every time the word digital creeps into a course title. Everything is digital, they say, and I sympathize. It is important here to refine our use of the term. Musical data in a digital state is inert until it is operated on by code. That code is also in a digital state. For people who write code that operates on music in a digital form, the delineation between data and processing is quite clear; no code in action, no sound. This book argues that it is time for a *code musicology* to provide analytical nuance and move beyond the metonymic use of "digital" in music analysis. Magnusson (2019) has discussed the need for a musicology of code to analyze compositions driven by computation, and here I suggest that needs to be expanded. The code behind the software that mediates so much human musical activity globally, is doing so much more than attending to locally bound technical needs, that the code as well as the infrastructure around it demands analysis.

Recent news events have reinforced the rise of code in other domains. The role of faulty software in the crashes of two Boeing 737 aircraft in 2018 and 2019 was a worrying alert to just how critical running code can be. Less tragic, but affecting many more people, was the Apple Facetime bug of January 2019. A 14-year-old discovered that it was possible to hear, and sometimes see, people who had been called using a group feature of the Facetime video communication application, but who had not actually answered the call (Perlroth 2019). Although a glaring invasion of privacy, Apple were slow in dealing with the issue when initially alerted numerous times by the youth's mother. A week or so later, after news of the fault went viral from a story on an Apple user website, the company disabled the group function, before releasing an update that fixed the bug. This all occurred not long after a statement by the Apple CEO reinforcing the supposed importance of privacy to the company. While this was a significant privacy breach, the manner in which the software update occurred is noteworthy. Someone at Apple released a code update via some sort of code-based web interface, that, within hours, was accessed by billions of people. That degree of centralization, focused in on a single piece of faulty code, while extraordinary, has become normalized. Google, through releasing code for the Android platform, is similar. These massive corporations, through their mechanisms of app store distribution centrally control access to software for billions of people. There are millions of apps, but only two main distribution mechanisms.

While the increasing power and influence of code on music is less drastic than a plane crash or global breach of privacy, the effects nevertheless demand attention. I argue for a code musicology to demonstrate that the effects of code on music are significant enough to warrant such attention and then bridge gaps in discipline knowledge. Music scholars will need to engage with how code and music connect, how that code is created, and under what circumstances and preconceptions. Writers of code will need to understand the broader, even global, implications their work might have as its effects on human music making grow and then broaden their understanding of musical practice beyond the Global North.

A code musicology builds a number of disciplinary bridges. One of these connects analysis of the operation and context of code with ethnomusicological work on music technology described as *technoculture*.[1] *Wired for Sound* is the main title of a collection of such work focusing attention on the technologies and processes involved in creating and circulating music (Greene and Porcello 2005). The editors use *wired* beyond the state of being electrical to include more complex ideas of conductivity and connectivity. Making music in this environment involves the "manipulation of electrical impulses" (1) and "In the contemporary paradigm the sound waves' measurements, rather than the sound waves themselves, travel across metal filaments as differentials in electrical charge, and sound information—also encoded as electrical charge—is manipulated by means of computer interfaces" (1). Assuming this refers to digital processes, then some stages have been skipped here. People manipulate computer interfaces which are themselves built of code which in turn directs code that manipulates signals that represent music. The interaction of electrical impulses occurring across these metal filaments represent running code and data. While at a very low level of hardware activity, these signals are essentially changes in electrical potential on microscopic wire-like pathways, it is more useful and comprehensible to consider the higher layers where manipulation occurs—code abstractions and associated structure. If following a wire is a valuable guide for thinking about how a musical signal is transformed, then following code is the corresponding guide in a digital environment. The *wired for sound* of Greene and Porcello (2005) would be *coded for sound* in a digital environment.

Another disciplinary bridge a code musicology makes is with the digital humanities. Berry (2011) describes a number of waves to comprehend the wide variety of work encompassed. The first focused on the use of digital tools such as databases and search engines, in an extension of traditional methods in the humanities. The second incorporated "born digital" media into the focus of research in the humanities. Berry (2011) has called for a third wave to explore code and software in digital humanities as part of a "computational turn." The proposed third wave is focused "around the underlying computationality of the forms held within a computational medium" (4), with the aim of looking at "the digital component of the digital humanities in the light of its medium specificity, as a way of thinking about how medial changes produce epistemic changes" (4). A code musicology is very much part of this third wave.

Running code, by its nature, involves decisions based on changing criteria; if this, then that, if not then this; loop over these instructions this many times, and so on. The combinations of numerous layers of code working together lead to effects that can be perceived as having a kind of agency. As Mackenzie (2006) points out: "If software matters, and if power, law and art are associated with software, then code as a material has become a significant way of distributing agency. Code is certainly not a unique involution of agency, but the patterns and permutations of agency that attach to it are particularly powerful and symptomatic" (8).

It might be argued that under ideal conditions this agency is always at the behest of its human creators, and that given all of the inputs and knowledge of the environment, the outputs should be able to be precisely and reliably predicted. The reality, however, is that those inputs, the number of layers of code in action, and the variety and intricacies of context means this is not the case. Code, and its operation in most modern contexts is extraordinarily complicated.

Disruption is a frequently invoked theme for many studies of music industries dealing with "the digital," "digitization," and "digitalization," despite the dominance of this domain for more than twenty years (Wikström and DeFilippi 2016; Daniel 2019; Moreau 2013; Hughes et al. 2016). One notable exception to this view is presented by Arditi (2015), who demonstrates that key music industry organizations and companies actively shaped the nature of music and related commerce in the digital domain. Analysis and discussion under the standard digital rubrics has also tended to ignore or at least bracket off the operation of code. Software, where discussed, is most often explored from the point of view of the interface between people and the program—the way people interact, rather than the underlying actions that ensue. Until relatively recently, these operations have not had effects useful to the broader projects of popular music studies and ethnomusicology. By this, I mean that matters of social context, politics, commerce, and analysis of musical texts had little to gain from a discussion of code in operation because the effects were local and largely technical in nature. If, for example, we are interested in the effects that easily shared small music files might have on industries based on duplicating and selling physical recordings, then the processes of mp3 conversion and associated minutiae of code operations do not matter, although the history and surrounding politics will.[2]

If, however, our focus of analysis is around privacy while listening to Spotify on a phone while wearing Bluetooth headphones, then things get far more complicated. Imagine a common example of using Spotify where we search for a song, or choose one from our library while online. First of all, those search terms go to Spotify's servers, possibly in another country. From where I write, beyond the personal data already held in association with my account, Spotify can collect my location, along with: URL information; online identifiers such as cookie data and IP addresses; information about the types of devices being used such as unique device IDs, network connection type, provider, network and device performance, browser type, language, information enabling digital rights management, operating system, and Spotify application version; device attributes of devices on a wifi network that are available to connect to the Spotify Service (such as speakers); non-precise location, which may be derived or inferred from certain technical data (IP address, language setting, or payment currency), to comply with geographic requirements in licensing agreements, deliver personalized content and advertising to you; and finally motion-generated or orientation-generated mobile sensor data for the purposes of providing specific Spotify features (Spotify 2019).

There is then an extraordinary list of things that we agree to let Spotify use our data for, among them marketing, promotion, advertising; compliance with legal obligations and law enforcement requests; fulfilling contractual obligations with third parties; conducting business planning, reporting, and forecasting; and conducting research, contests, surveys, and sweepstakes (Spotify 2019). When my request is processed, an encrypted stream of data is sent back, to be decrypted by the Spotify software on my device. More data can be collected as I play the song, including possible movements I may make if listening on a phone! Audio data is then sent wirelessly to my headphones. If I have the Bose Connect app installed, and have not expressly chosen to block data being sent out, Bose can get data about location, time, and song metadata, until finally conversion takes place and the familiar effects of changes in air pressure make it to me as music.

While it is generally unnecessary to understand the intricate working detail of code, having some means of discussing operations at a higher level is important, and this book offers some ideas and models for that. In many circumstances, the code we run every day is hidden from us, even if we would like to see it, because it is 'closed source' or proprietary. The actual workings are known only to those with access to the source code, and that number can be relatively small. I use Linux as my daily computing environment, and although almost all of the software I use is open source, it takes some effort to actually see it. Even then, specialized skills are required to know what it might do. Kitchin and Dodge (2011), in exploring code from the perspective of human geography, quote Rosenberg (2008) in an amusing twist on the Battle of Britain quote: "The art of creating software continues to be a dark mystery, even to the experts. Never in history have we depended so completely on a product that so few know how to make well" (23).

It is also obscure in terms of the reticence of scholars in the humanities, even the technologically adept, to engage with code directly. For many in the humanities, software design and analysis has been the domain of colleagues in the sciences. Marino (2020) has mapped out a critical code studies to guide exploration as "an approach to code studies that applies critical hermeneutics to the interpretation of computer code, program architecture, and documentation within a sociohistorical context" (59). This book aims to apply relevant aspects of such an approach to musical contexts and practices.

I pilot readers through some aspects of code and its contexts by drawing on my own software development experience. In 2012, I started developing a simple audio recording app that allowed me to overdub recordings over an existing track, then add—"bounce," in recording parlance—that recording to a master track, and repeat to build up a multi-track recording. The idea stemmed from my use of multi-track cassette recording devices of the mid-1980s aimed at a nascent amateur music recording scene. I called the app Twotrack and released it to the Google Play app store. Since then, almost half a million people have downloaded the app from over 150 countries. On any given day, hundreds of people use it, all over the world. I will discuss this in more detail later, but throughout this process, I gained access to a considerable quantity of anonymized data as to where the app was being used, when and for how long, crash reports, and so on. Users could provide ratings, reviews, and I could respond, tweak the app, and update it. A quotidian, supposedly simple act of personal recording and listening has become an exercise in data collection involving three corporations, tightly bound to the commercial logic of modern online advertising.

One of the main aims of the book is to demystify this domain for those exploring music from perspectives such as ethnomusicology, popular music studies, media studies, and cultural studies. This will involve connecting those aspects of software studies that have relevancy for music under two main ideas, 'the life of code,' and the 'life around code.' It is important to make a distinction between the terms code and software. By code, I refer to the range of human readable representations of instructions that are carried out by computing hardware. By software I refer to the broader category of lower-level instructions, not necessarily readable by humans, that has been compiled or interpreted. Software is also used as a noun to describe the sorts of programs people download, buy, or share.

As Kitchin and Dodge (2011) point out: "Software then is not an immaterial, stable, and neutral product. Rather, it is a complex, multifaceted, mutable set of relations created through diverse sets of discursive, economic, and material practices" (37).

I explore case studies to provide examples of the kinds of insights that a code focused study can provide. This is organized into three main areas: effects on aesthetics and implications for future music making; how code libraries, code structures and the business and scenes of writing it constrain and delimit possibilities for making music; and how code in operation stemming from the infrastructure in which it is created affects power relationships and drives imbalance in the global context.

BOOK STRUCTURE

Chapters 1 and 2 aim to demystify code, explore the context of making it, and connect scholarship in software studies with relevant concepts for music. The mediation of music by software is multidimensional in that it involves both technical and social elements. Software can be thought of as having a lifecycle, in the sense that it is created, it is developed, tested, modified, and works in relationship with other software and hardware. It often has a finite life span, or serves as an ancestor for subsequent versions of itself. There is biological and cultural life around software; people write it in specific contexts at certain times for particular reasons. That life is usually highly social and discursive, and enmeshes with the politics of commerce, power, diversity, and intellectual property. For the section dealing with the life of code, I unpack relevant material that is often covered under the term "digitization." This involves definitions, a discussion of ontology, and relationships between how music organizes time and how code organizes time. A historical perspective opens the section on the life around code, drawing out parallels between histories of computing and music studio recording. Although the digitization of music did not occur on a widespread basis until late in the 20th century, and thus the history of music and computer technology are out of phase to some extent, once we zoom out, interesting patterns and connections emerge.

The chapter on code and constraints delves into instructions, algorithms, rules and decisions, and how the libraries and languages in which they are constructed constrain, moderate, and delimit musical possibilities. Although the digitization of music has led to a variety of genres that build on the affordances provided by manipulation of music in the time domain, the processing of digitized audio, and its relationship to notions of music and human time are complicated. A section is therefore devoted to an examination of time in relation to code abstractions required once music has been digitized. A number of languages have been developed for the creation of music since the 1950s, and how they have influenced thinking about music creation with computers, and how they afford certain possibilities, and constrain others is explored. Software applications are built from a selection of code libraries that have been developed to enable functions so that individual coders do not have to individually reinvent the wheel. These provide quite specific constraints and affordances in relation to music and provoke a number of questions.

Code directly affects musical aesthetics; it can emulate, copy, extend, and create new sonic possibilities. The code and aesthetics chapter looks at digital emulation of analog musical instruments and equipment, the live coding scene, glitch and game music. A number of questions are posed. What are the affordances of code that generate new approaches to music? What effort is put into modeling and rebuilding aesthetics associated with an analog world and what does this tell us? What do musics that emanate from 'user' or player interaction tell us about possible musical futures?

The rise of code leads to shifts in power through the way agency, communication, and centralization works under the code centered environment we increasingly operate in. This is explored through an app case study from a development perspective using the app called *Twotrack* I have developed and released. People, and now sometimes machines, write code from particular perspectives under certain contexts for a range of reasons. As machines listen, data gets collected, organized, and connected, and as AI is increasingly used, what kind of power gets vested in the machines themselves, and what kind of relationships does this mean for both those who write the code, those who run the software, and those who use it?

These phenomena are not limited to the always connected population of the Global North. Since the 1990s I have been conducting ethnomusicological research into the music of Papua New Guinea, a nation often (mistakenly) constructed as exotic, remote, and marginal. My interest there has usually involved music technology, from guitars to cell phones.[3] From about 2007, it was clear that cellphones, tablets, and laptops were transforming how people made, shared, and listened to music. This was part of a far more widespread phenomenon throughout the Global South. Further, changes that were taking decades to occur in the Global North were taking place in much more compressed periods of time, providing acute analytical insights. Software, and the code underlying it, is mediating more and more musical activities for a growing proportion of humanity. Chapter 6 poses questions such as where do power imbalances lie when code mediates musical practices globally? What does this mean for gender and cultural diversity? This draws on experiences from another app I have developed that serves as a case study from the Global South "developing for the next billion," to borrow Google's phrase. The conclusion collates a number of key tenets to codify our code musicology and offers some suggestions for practical action in concert with an existing music technology manifesto widely supported by scholars and practitioners in the field.

NOTES

1. See, for example, Lysloff and Gay (2003; Lysloff 1997; Théberge 1997; Gay 1998; Perlman 2003; Meintjes 2003; Porcello 2004; Bates 2010; Crowdy 2007).
2. See, for example, Sterne (2012).
3. See (Crowdy (2016, 2007, 2015).

Chapter One

The Life of Code

The aim of this chapter is to demystify code by exploring relevant aspects of its ontology. This exposes how processes of abstraction and coding in digital environments become intertwined in musical practices, aesthetics, values, and traditions. First, I want to place the overused term "digitization" in perspective, then relegate it to the background where it belongs.

For the purposes of this book, I employ a relatively narrow definition of digitization, focused on the process of transformation of signals from analog to digital. This avoids confusion around the more catch-all uses of the term often invoked in studies of music. Perhaps a more nuanced approach to talking about these wider meanings is taken by Hesmondhalgh and Meier (2018) who use the term "digitalisation." More commonly found in business and industry contexts, it is used to help describe the larger processes at play in the digital domain. Many in popular music studies and cultural studies have used "digitisation" in the same way. Hesmondhalgh and Meier (2018) describe key moments and processes as "the rise of internet-linked file-sharing and later peer-to-peer technologies," "the integration of copy-protection systems into coherently combined play-back and retail interfaces, based on the PC plus iPod/MP3 player," and "the popularisation of streaming services, especially as mobile apps…based on mobile phones, laptops and tablets." These verbs—rise, integrate, and popularise—all operate on objects that are essentially complicated aggregations of code. These specific examples are excellent illustrations of why the actions taking place within those aggregations, and a discussion of the affordances and constraints that delimit the possibilities of their actions demand examination in their own right due to their myriad effects on aesthetics, musical practices, and associated industrial and power relationships. While "digitalisation" is a term that better encapsulates both process as action through code, and medial state as a data stream of digits, it is not a term I will use. A key goal of this book is to pull apart the processes acting on music as data in a digital state, and tease out approaches to the study of the actions underway, to reveal some fundamental ongoing changes in music, surrounding practices and politics. To begin, there are some critical qualities of the state of digitization—music as digital data—that requires some initially technical, but valuable explanation as we work out more complex contexts and activities.

Computers demand data in a digital format.[1] Digitization is a process, a way of representing a signal that is continuous in time, such as an electrical signal, in numbers. An analog musical signal refers to the representation of sound once it has been transduced from variations in pressure in the air, by a microphone, to corresponding fluctuations in voltage of an electrical current. Numerical samples of the voltage are taken at regular time intervals, known as the sampling rate. The simplest and most common digital format is simply a stream of numbers representing relative amplitude at regularly spaced points in time. The common audio format used in CDs, for example, consists of a series of 16 bit binary numbers with an integer range of 65536. These have been sampled at a rate of 44,100 each second, so there are 44,100 numbers for each second of audio.[2] There is no point to digitization in and of itself. Things are digitized so they can be processed by code—read, modified, copied/cloned, moved. To hear it back as sound, it must be read, ordered by code, then fed to a chip that can convert those numbers back into a continuously varying voltage, to be sent to an amplifier, and ultimately a speaker that transduces it back to pressure waves in air.

Once in a digital state and stored in a computer (and I include smartphones and tablets in this definition), these numbers are not always stored sequentially as they might be on a CD. This state bears some exploration, as it illustrates how much work is being done in the domain of code to provide us with ways to interpret our digital data as humans in an order and at a rate that we can perceive as music. Data, whether audio or something else, is presented to users through the metaphor of a file; a coherent digital object. Data on a hard drive, however, is often stored noncontiguously to compensate for how the read/write mechanism works. An addressing system then keeps track of where different blocks are placed to reconstruct the sequence coherently (Allen-Robertson 2017, 461). Although this makes sense from an engineering perspective at the scale of hard drive operation, in human terms it would be like taking a printout of something we had written, chopping it into hundreds or thousands of pieces, then storing them individually in different places, out of order, all the while noting this down. When we need to access that information again, we get our notes, find all of the individual pieces and glue them together in the order we wrote the words in the first place. Computers are many magnitudes of order faster at this sort of thing than humans, of course, which is what makes such an operation practical in a code environment.

A common state of music represented in digital form is therefore one of chronic fragmentation. This is not the case for other forms of storage such as solid-state drives (SSDs), but code is still needed to reconstitute common data formats such as mp3. In these cases, data has been encoded in chunks that need to be decoded to create a coherent stream for musical purposes. Without code there is no musical chronology. This is significant for a form which unfolds in time, and in a sense organizes human perceptions of time. It is just as easy to present digital musical data in a random, or modified order, as it is to present it in the order it was recorded in. While we tend to think of music in digital formats in the form of files or a stream, these are phantasms generated on the fly by low level code connecting information about data order with the actual locations of sets of sequences of numbers on physical digital storage. This helps explain why music in this particular computer-based digital domain affords manipulation in time to an extent no previous medium has. As this book will demonstrate, when we shift our focus to what is going on in code we see the extraordinary effort that goes in to the coding of abstractions to reconcile continuous musical time, with discrete machine time.

With recorded music, there have always been relationships between storage media, the sound of reproduction, and musical creativity. Vinyl records have time length limitations due to their physical nature; there is constant low-level noise, and occasional pops and crackles. If scratched, skips, even loops can occur. There is no way of changing the order of musical output within a particular track, although speed can be changed and the needle can be scrubbed back and forth for sonic effect. Tape allows much longer recordings and also has constant noise, but with its own particular sonic profile. It is possible to edit tape, and as a result change the order of musical events but it is a time-consuming, labor-intensive process. Forward thinking artists experimented with cutting up tape and re-ordering it for musical purposes from the 1960s, but the complicated and painstaking process involved points to the fact that the media did not easily afford such manipulation; it was much easier to keep the tape together. In all cases, certain aesthetic associations with particular media have spawned creativity and new tools for new sounds, effects, and genres, from scratching vinyl, to tape compression emulation plugins, tape loops, and so on. Digital formats have also been part of this, with the glitches from errors in CD playback forming the basis for new genres, for example.

CDs are an important point of transition for a code musicology. In storing digital data in a spiral from the center out to the edge, they were the last mass adopted physical digital media before hard drives where data was stored sequentially. Secondly, the incorporation of CD readers (and eventually writers) into home and office computers through the 1990s, meant they were the main source for the widespread movement of music to storage types integral to computing. I would like to spend some time marking out the moment when the physical storage of music shifts from being in an order that matches its sequential order in time, to being in a state of fracture as just described. This serves as a critical point to grasp what this particular storage focused nuance of "the digital" represents for music.

To think through this, I turn to work by Kirschenbaum (2008) exploring the nature of digital texts and their materiality through a grammatology of the hard drive. Kirschenbaum explores the materiality of digital texts through analysis of the hard drive to argue for better ways to fathom media in digital forms. Kirschenbaum (2008) counteracts what he describes as a "medial ideology" that has built up through writing that sees electronic, digital text as ephemeral, transient, and not inscribed (36). Two ideas, *forensic* materiality, and *formal* materiality, are presented to help conceptually apprehend the layers that combine and interact in digital texts. Forensic materiality refers to how the individual can be discerned in material traces, and therefore how ideas of the autographic can be applied to digital texts. Under very high magnification, for example, it is possible to discern physical differences between individual bits on a hard drive as "The bits themselves prove strikingly autographic, all of them similar but no two exactly alike, each displaying idiosyncracies and imperfections—in much the same way that conventional letter forms, both typed and handwritten, assume their own individual personality under extreme magnification" (Kirschenbaum 2008, 62).

While we have largely moved to different kinds of devices such as SSDs, these too have forensic qualities. How is it then, that if I share an mp3 file with someone, they get an exact clone? Kirschenbaum, focusing on text, draws on the notions of the allographic; it does not matter if individual bits that combine to represent a particular letter differ, what matters is that we end up seeing the desired letter, not something else. The same applies for mp3 data. As long as the numbers in its data sequence end up being represented correctly, forensic differences are simply interesting material traces and reminders of digital materiality. Most importantly for my purposes, however, this interface between the autographic and allographic marks a moment where code is the mediator. Following Kirschenbaum, code created from abstractions to re-create music for humans from numbers for machines can be an example of formal materiality:

> My word processor presents me with a certain document model, and while its formal behaviors ultimately come to rest in the forensic materiality of chips, memory, and other aspects of the hardware configuration, much of what we tend to essentialize about new media is in fact merely the effect of a particular set

of social choices implemented and instantiated in the formal modelling of the digital environments in question. (133)

It is the abstract layer largely represented by code in this example that could be categorized as formal materiality following Kirschenbaum. For most people engaging with music in digital forms, while we imagine sequentially organized files or streams via the internet, our view is "optimized and impoverished, a partial and simplistic window onto the diverse electronic records that have accumulated on the surface of the magnetic disk" (53).

In an analysis of hard drives and their materiality, Allen-Robertson (2017) argues that "a technology's affordances arise from an interplay of forensic and formal materialities and . . . 'digital media' is no different" (467). I want to build from that and think about the interface between forensic and formal materiality and what it means for music. I do this to expose two mutually interacting phenomena. The first is to show how aspects of the digitally forensic percolate into our awareness as users and user-musicians. The sound of the CD glitch is a good example here. Differences on the surface of a CD engage error correction software that results in a particular sonic effect. Artists then use those sounds in new forms of music, in similar ways to how technology has been used or misused, depending on perspective, throughout the history of music technology. The second phenomena is when those aesthetic practices and values then get abstracted and coded through processes of formal materiality. To continue with the glitch example, plugins for music production software have been developed that re-create those sounds through code. Musical values, in historical context, within the affordances and constraints of current hardware and software, are written in code. Values get coded.

The genre known as Chiptune provides another useful example (Paul 2014). Hardware in early personal computers had limitations that provided constraints on the timbre and number of voices available for computer games on such platforms. The resultant sounds have formed the basis for a genre of music that is now created on machines without such constraints. Code is written to emulate those constraints to re-create the desired sounds. The aesthetic values of that genre are then available now, and for the future. Code is a great deal easier to replicate than the original hardware. There are also cases where sounds and associated aesthetics that get coded have their origins in the analog world, rather than the digital. This will be examined in a later discussion on how various older technologies, such as guitar amplifiers, studio equipment, even microphones, get emulated digitally. That the sonic origin of these examples do not have digital origins speaks to one of the important ideas that this approach to analysis reveals, and that is about how the digital plays a role in musical continuity, and how it sustains certain production traditions.

Knowing what to look at in the materiality of digital technology, and when, is a critical part of this proposed code musicology. Hayles (2004) provides a useful reminder about this when considering the impact of materiality in a digital environment on texts as part of a media specific analysis: "I can think of many contemporary electronic works that foreground the interplay between natural language and computer code . . . but I know of no work that foregrounds the computer's power cord" (71). When effects of materiality percolate into realms of value for music, whether aesthetic or power-related, we should have the tools at our disposal to take notice, and recognize the irrelevant and fruitless sites of examination, represented by Hayles here through the power cord.

A look at the history of code and software in music firstly shows the historical connections between music and the digital technologies that extend far beyond more recent narratives of digital disruption centered on commercial music industries. While I do not discount the usefulness of disruption as it has been used in relation to commerce, a code musicology helps us locate important instances as to how the digital fits into a historical continuum. The perspective of code rather than widespread digitization of music places digital technologies along the same spectrum of technology use as other music technology, from acoustic instruments to analog synthesizers. There are numerous musical practices that value unique sounds that have emerged from digital hardware. As hardware has changed, those sounds then need to be emulated in software and, as a result, become part of sustained musical genres and traditions. This connects to the widespread phenomenon of emulating analog aesthetics such as the sound of a guitar amp through software. This also extends beyond the sonic, shown by the active curation of continuity from an analog domain through the encoding of practices such as turning a representation of a knob. We see musical values and associated practices being coded, and then sustained through the use of code-based tools we recognize as software.

The most in-depth work looking at how music software, interfaces, and associated practices shape music, electronic music in particular, is by Magnusson (2019) and D'Errico (2016) with the idea of "interface aesthetics." Other studies to examine software interfaces and communities of users include Strachan (2017) and Bell (2018). These analyses of interface design, associated practices by users, and sonic signatures are a critical locus, stepping stones even, for the move to examine code more explicitly. While we generally think of software, at least initially, through the interface we interact with, that interface, and the elements we click on, type into, mouse over and so on, are built from code. They are visual, sonic, and sometimes tactile results of code in operation; pixels are rendered, audio buffers filled, signals are sent to a phone component that vibrates. Kitchin and Dodge reinforce the importance of looking at this underlying code: "this proposed study requires analysis to be concentrated on software itself and not simply the first-order impacts of software-enabled technology. All too often, studies focus on such technologies, ignoring the critical role played by code in shaping their technicity and unfolding solutions to problems" (Kitchin and Dodge 2011, 260).

Interfaces represent a particular abstraction, often modeled on preexisting practices and associated technologies called skeuomorphs (Bell, Hein, and Ratcliffe 2015). We need to add to analyses based on interfaces for a number of reasons. These include constraints, affordances, agency, and the side-effects of code. It is therefore necessary to delve a bit deeper into the actual nature of code, and explore what type of thing it is.

Although code is stored in a format indistinguishable from other digital data as a sequence of numbers, at its highest level of abstraction it is text. For those with access to it, it is readable. This can be at a variety of levels, from what is known as machine code or assembly language that represents instructions to a CPU, to more readable higher-level languages with words and syntax for assigning variables, data structures, decision making, looping, and so on. Depending on the language, code is either compiled into a machine readable format, then run, or is interpreted on the fly. Different languages have structural features that enable particular approaches to implementing algorithms and directing the flow of execution. Only the simplest of programs is ever really just a single file; more often programs are broken into numerous chunks that reference each other. Although readable from left to right, top to bottom, the actual process of visualizing the flow of instructions can be labyrinthine. Languages are chosen depending on the purpose at hand, and different skills may be required. There is a considerable difference in skill and experience needed between writing assembly code as part of a device driver for an audio interface, and writing Sonic Pi code to generate a tone, for example.

Code, once in operation, is dynamic, and although generally designed to be predictable, the circumstances encountered by running code often leads to faults known as bugs. Indeed, reporting, prioritizing, fixing bugs, and releasing modified versions is a significant part of the coding process. Although as users we become aware of such faults as our activities are interrupted, the offending circumstances and unexpected flow of code execution is obscured; we see bugs mediated through unwanted interfaces such as a disappearing window replaced by an error message in another window, or an endlessly cycling visual progress icon. This mediation is also true of code when operating as expected, as Mackenzie (2006) points out: "What is visible to a programmer working on a piece of software may be almost totally invisible to users, who only see code mediated through an interface or some change in their environment: the elevator arrives, the television changes channels, the telephone rings" (13).

A great deal of the code that is operating for most people much of the time is not readable by everyone. Closed source software like this is accessed by developers and those in the company creating and distributing it; that is where their value for financial purposes lie. This is at the core of a methodological problem when considering code. We can analyze the way an audio waveform is rendered in open-source software like the digital audio workstation (DAW) Ardour, but not in examples where the source is not available (ProTools, for example).

Code is fundamentally non-rivalrous (Chun 2011, 37). Rivalrous is a term used in economics to differentiate between physical goods and those such as digital files that may be copied (cloned, really) effectively without real cost, and the associated potential (or not) for commerce. If I take your CD away, you have one less CD. If you send me an electronic copy in the form of mp3 files, it can be done with no loss to you. Dealing with this has been an ongoing series of challenges for music commerce, from mp3s and the challenge to physical media business models, to streaming services, effectively removing user/consumer access to the non-rivalrous good, and charging as a service. The non-rivalrous nature of software can be more complex. While open-source software can be freely packaged or bundled and distributed to be copied, approaches to deter copying such as encryption, obfuscation, copy protection using hardware USB "keys," registration, and subscription are common.

Before discussing the life cycle of code and associated systems, it is worth briefly clarifying that terms like "copy" and "move" in relation to digital data are really convenient ideas we borrow from our experiences of physical versions of music. For copying, the term "clone" is probably more apt, in that the copy is identical to the original; indeed the idea of original becomes open to question. The idea of moving data is also just a convenience, as data is essentially cloned to another location, and the original deleted. Further, the code that actually carries out these cloning and deletion operations is itself stored in the same format, and is able to be operated on in exactly the same way.

Frequently, code-based systems are described by one of the most complex glosses there is—life. In a frank memoir of working in software engineering, Ullman (1997) recounts experiences of the social, often messy business of managing and building systems through her role as a software engineer and manager of software engineers. It is a rare and insightful self-reflexive insider view that addresses the politics at play in software development. Ullman (1997) describes software as having a life: "We say it has a 'life cycle':

from birth, to productive maturity, to bug-filled old age" (116). Often, that life exceeds that of hardware. Consider Apple and its central music program, iTunes. iTunes was introduced to Apple computers in 2001, developed out of a program called SoundJam MP written by developer Bill Kincaid. It was subsequently adapted to run on iPods, iPads, iPhones, watches, and a continuous series of laptop and desktop computers. While that software is not visible in the same way as the objects in which it resides, without it, the objects would not function as intended. Kitchin and Dodge (2011) offer the neologism "codeject" to reinforce the essential role of software in such situations; these objects are simply not functional without code. All of these Apple devices are codejects; without running code they are mere shells. The fact that we can sit down and interact with the same physical object irrespective of whether we are filing our tax returns or mixing a dance track reinforces the crucial idea that differentiation lies in the software being used, and thus the code we bring into operation.

Code and associated systems can be complex. Ullman points out how some systems that have had many programmers work on them over a long period are in fact not even really understandable by individuals anymore. Consider this description of a mainframe system she had worked on that was 16 years old, had 96 programmers working on it before her, and was nearing the end of its life cycle:

> By the time a computer system becomes old, no one completely understands it. A system made out of old junky technology becomes, paradoxically, precious. It is kept running but as if in a velvet box: open it carefully, just look, don't touch.
> The preciousness of an old system is axiomatic. The longer the system has been running, the greater the number of programmers who have worked on it, the less any one person understands it. As years pass and untold numbers of programmers and analysts come and go, the system takes on a life of its own. It runs. That is its claim to existence: it does useful work. However badly, however buggy, however obsolete—it runs. And no one individual completely understands how. Its very functioning demands we stop treating it as some mechanism we've created like, say, a toaster, and start to recognize it as a being with a life of its own. We have little choice anyway: we no longer control it. We have two choices: respect it or kill it. (117)

An application like iTunes which has been in constant development since 2001, no doubt contains code now that was written then. Even if not, it is an aggregate that has slowly morphed as parts are changed, added, deleted. Software is a packaged result of changes in code made by numerous people over time. Code has life around it as people write it, get it running, fix it, redesign it, and so on. Those people have constraints, ideas about the world, as well as different skills and experiences. What is central for this book is how these values, constraints, affordances, all embedded in particular cultural, social, and historical circumstances, relate to the aggregate we know as music.

As a way of thinking about complex, multifaceted aggregates operating within digital environments, and making digital environments operate, Mackenzie (2006) uses the notion of "variable ontology." Java, for example, although defined as a computer language in the dictionary: ". . . is not so much a single thing, object or media, but an unfolding, bifurcating, loosely held ensemble of practices, imaginings, logos, knowledges and artifacts" (95).

Music is similar, and can be thought of as "a multiplicity of practices that includes music theory, instrument design, composition, publishing, pedagogy, communicating cultures, media, economies, science, and engineering" (Magnusson 2019, 8). Given this, what then happens when one variable ontology meets another? In subsequent chapters I will show examples of how both change, and how analyses of the intricacies of such intersecting processes are crucial as the significance and extent of musical activities in such environments continues to grow. A code-focused musicology will be shown to offer some rich material from which to consider music. Fortunately, there are some examples from domains other than music that provide useful guides.

Montfort et al. (2014) develop an entire book from discussion of a single line of code to explore intersections between visual art and code. This one-liner, an example of a particular genre of coding, was written for an early hobbyist computer in the early 1980s—the Commodore 64—and when run, creates a maze-like pattern on the screen:

TEXTBOX 1.1: 10 PRINT CODE ONE LINER

```
10 Print Chr$(205. 5+rnd(1)); : Goto 10
```

Each element of the line of code is examined in detail and used as a departure point for discussions about art, graphics, random numbers, and the historical and social context in which the code was written. Software and hardware are part of the contextual mesh, and different historical periods are explored through discussions of ports of the program to other computers and languages. As Montfort et al. (2014) points out: "10 PRINT was selected as the focus of this book not because the program sits at the summit of all possible one-liners in any language and for any platform, but because the program can lead the way to appreciating code and the contexts in which it emerges, circulates, and operates" (262).

For music, a code musicology must at some stage connect code and sound. Uniquely digital operations and side-effects have created sonic opportunities that have resulted in some distinctly digital traces of sound in particular styles. Brøvig-Hanssen and Danielsen (2016) explore this sound, creating what they describe as digital signatures. They point out how "a given technology affords particular possibilities to the consumer, in terms of enabling as well as constraining particular functions" (15). Like Strachan (2017) and others, they focus on the affordances provided by the interfaces between users and code:

> This visual representation of the music now arguably influences how we compose it in the first place. For instance, using the cursor to drag and drop chunks of "music" across the timeline of the arrange window encourages us to think about music as consisting of bits and fragments that can be easily shuffled around, rather than as a continuous flow that evolves organically through time. (14)

That interface is constituted by code, and when we compare this scenario with the one of processing chunks of audio data, there is a connection between how easy it is to move chunks of data around with how easy it is to represent that in a visual interface.

Luckily for most of us, the intricate details get sorted out by software engineers, and the musical things musicians want to do are enabled through complex layers of code. That is the point though; as this code mediates more of our global musical activity, and the engineering sets limits and opens up possibilities, being more engaged with those processes is incumbent upon people with understanding, hopes, and experience in the musics on which this code increasingly encroaches.

The fact that code gets processed in some sort of sequence in time is significant. What is also important here is that sequence order can be modified by code instruction, dependent on particular situations and circumstances—the world of "if–then," for example. Redhead (2015) argues convincingly that "recorded formats of music are emerging into fluid forms." There are precedents for this throughout art music, with aleatoric experiments, and various computer music examples. DJ practice also speaks to this more fluid, malleable idea of what music is or might be becoming or can be. That has an obvious difference to older ways of thinking about music as a given, set text. If, as is commonly stated, the media influences the kind of music that gets made, then it will be in the details of how that media operates that many of the possibilities—probabilities even—lie. That operation is brought into action through code created by people in particular circumstances, and it is that I turn to in more detail in the next chapter.

NOTES

1. There are such things as analog computers, which do not demand data in a digital format, but they are highly specialized, rare devices not relevant to the discussion here.

2. This is for a mono signal—the size is doubled for stereo which consists of two channels; one for the left side, one for the right side.

Chapter Two

Life around Code

One of the most valuable assertions from the one-liner study of Montfort et al. (2014) is that "programming is culturally situated just as computers are culturally situated, which means that the study of code should be no more ahistorical than the study of any cultural text" (262). Here I want to map out intertwined histories of computing and music from the 1950s and indicate important changes that have occurred as code has become more significant in musical lives. The aim here is to reinforce ideas of digital connection over disruption. As Magnusson (2019) reminds us, digital instruments "are hybrid systems whose histories, ideologies, embodied performance, musicologies, aesthetics, and styles originate in practices that are pre-digital, often with cultural patterns that can be traced back centuries into our musical past" (xi).

This assists in understanding the rise in the prominence and role of software and code for music. It also exposes changes in roles and activities for making and sharing music. This in turn helps us to explore changes in the politics of power and cultural capital underlying these shifts. I look at this primarily through a lens of professional versus amateur practices. In reinforcing the longevity of ties between code and music, we can see how musical aesthetics and activities demonstrate longer connections that contrast to discourses of disruption that dominate popular music narratives.

INTERTWINED HISTORIES

Some interesting parallels emerge between the histories of computing and studio music production from the 1950s through the 1980s. Both fields featured large electronic devices located in specially designed spaces operated by engineers with particular expertise. Both drew on electronic technology emerging from the Second World War. Both used tape for storage for many years, although tape in music production remained in the analog domain until well into the 1980s. Very early computers used vacuum tubes as the main switching devices. Music technology also incorporated vacuum tubes, primarily for amplification. Interestingly, music is one of the only fields that still uses such "tubes," as they are commonly referred to, for high end studio equipment and guitar amplifiers (Barbour 1998). Tubes are used for the sound they impart as a result of harmonic distortion in an audio processing chain and are revered for perceptions of what is now described as "warmth" in the resultant sound.

The widespread digitization of music did not take place until computing power and storage became adequate and cost effective in the years surrounding the turn of the 21st century. The digital relationship between code and music, however, stretches back a great deal further. One of the earliest direct associations between sound and electronic computing was the loudspeaker connected to the Australian serial computer CSIRAC in 1951 and set up to sound out program instructions. CSIRAC programmer Trevor Pearcey recounted how the speaker was first used to identify problems with programs. Pearcey described how a change in the rhythm of the clicks emanating from the speaker could alert programmers to a fault in execution (Doornbusch 2018). Later, the musical potential of this device was explored through programming the machine to generate diatonic tones and sequencing a number of simple melodies (Doornbusch 2004).

More serious, dedicated musical work through the 1950s involving the creation of a computer language for music by Max Mathews is well documented, and will be discussed in more detail later. This led to the growth of a number of influential experimental studios associated with institutions in the US and Europe that were critical sites for the emergence of computer and electroacoustic music and the development of electronic music technology (Manning 2004, 386–87).

Although musician-academics used computers to make music from the earliest days of computing, mainstream music recording and early computing were essentially parallel developments with little interaction. The moment that computing and the recording industries really started to connect was through early digital recordings of classical music made by the Soundstream company, led by engineer Thomas Stockham. Stockham was motivated by a desire to reduce noise, and won numerous awards for his work. Stockham's son, in an interview recorded by the Audio Engineering Society (AES) describes how his father had claimed from as early as the 1950s that music and images would one day be digital (Audio Engineering Society 2000). He described this as being widely regarded as a "crackpot" view at the time. By the early 1970s, however, Soundstream was making commercial recordings of orchestras using PDP11 computers and digital tape.

Sony had also developed digital audio recording devices in the early 1970s and gained professional studio uptake with a two-track digital recorder in 1978, then a 24-track digital recorder in 1981 (Sony, n.d.). Digital devices for processing sound in the studio were also developed in the late 1970s. Eventide were pioneers in this with a digital delay released in 1971, and from the mid-1970s a series of harmonizers. AMS was another company building digital delays, reverb units, and digital consoles from the late 1970s. Computer automation of studio consoles was another area of digital innovation from the mid-1980s. The lack of computing speed and high cost of storage kept the digitization of audio highly specialized until at least the early 1980s, however.

One of the most significant developments in digital technology was that of sampling. The Fairlight Computer Music Instrument (CMI) is one of the most famous, and allowed sounds to be sampled, then played back at different pitches in editable sequences (Harkins 2019, 2015). Designed in Australia, the Fairlight cost the equivalent of a modest Sydney house at the time, resulting in their use mainly by wealthy musicians, and some studios. Software had to be written specifically for such devices. The makers of the Fairlight bought the source code of an operating system used for medical equipment, then modified it to become its custom operating system. While the Fairlight was out of reach to most people, the world of computing was becoming much more available for a wider population in the Global North, if not very useful for musicians at first.

Early personal computers were initially aimed at hobbyists interested in programming, and it took many years for computing power and storage capability to meet the speeds and sizes necessary to process and store music digitally. I got my first personal computer as a teenager in 1980. It was a Sinclair ZX-80, had 1kb of RAM, a processor running at 3.25MHz, and programs were saved and loaded using an audio cassette. One second of audio data at CD quality takes up more than 40 times the size of RAM that this tiny computer had. I was an active musician at the time, but its limitations meant that the idea of it being used for recording music was beyond my imagination. Computers were being used more actively in music education, however. As an undergraduate music student in the mid-1980s, for example, we used a computer for ear training, with a system known as GUIDO (Hofstetter 1981), and although a great deal seemed to made of its cutting edge status in music education and considerable cost, I recoiled at first hearing the plain expressionless tones that were offered in dictation and recognition exercises. More imaginative timbres were coded for games written for early hobbyist computers, and this will be discussed in more detail later.

Although beyond the scope of discussion here, synthesizers from the late 1970s included various digital elements, from microprocessors for storage of patches to digital approaches to synthesis. These devices all had low level code running in them. As such instruments became more prevalent, in 1983 a group of digital instrument manufacturers agreed on and published a protocol for inter-machine communication, the Musical Instrument Digital Interface (MIDI). As processing power and storage density continued to increase, music and computing became more tightly bound as a result of MIDI interfaces allowing data to flow back and forth between synthesizers and computers. Early home computer models such as those by Atari and Amiga allowed accurate sequencing, and sophisticated software such as "Notator" emerged to enable this. MIDI is control data, and thus requires a great deal less computing power and storage capability to operate than digitized audio. As both consumer and commercial computing narrowed to two main operating systems, Microsoft's Windows and Apple's MacOS, older software was ported and new software written with sequencing and tracking capabilities, catering for a growing market of professional and amateur music producers.[1]

Recording studios remained analog, using multi-track tape formats until the 1990s with the introduction of ADAT. These were standalone machines that recorded to S-VHS tape digitally and could be chained together for up to 128 tracks of audio. Mix magazine points out how costs for 24 track recording went from an estimated USD$150,000 to USD$12,000, almost overnight (Petersen 2010). Although ADAT was digital, it used a tape machine-like interface and controller. Innovative technology companies such as NeXT computing developed powerful, media focused computers and associated GUI software. NeXT developed machines and software in the late 1980s with built-in Digital Signal Processing (DSP) and CD quality audio. The development of a range of sound cards for computers through the 1990s was significant in allowing ordinary office and personal devices to record and play music with relative ease at high standards of audio quality. Allied to this was the inclusion of CD ROM drives that could play audio CDs, and subsequent software that could 'rip' this digital data, encode it as mp3, and store it on the computer's hard drive. As computer systems improved in capability, hard disk-based systems such as ProTools entered the professional studio, along with their associated visualization of waveforms and editing capabilities. Hard disk recording using various DAWs—many of which are still being developed today—expanded rapidly on Apple's computers, and later Windows-based machines.

As Chadabe (1997, 200) points out, the music software industry really began forming in the 1980s. In its early stages it consisted of individuals and small groups of people creating software for specific purposes (MIDI control, sequencing, sampling, recording and so on) and specific devices. DAW software was developed and spread as personal computing power and storage improved, and its impact on music production has been mapped out by Strachan (2017) and Bell (2018) among others. Chadabe describes Steinberg Research's early work on the DAW Cubase as laying essential foundations, followed by a variety of similar tools, including the widely used 'Pro-Tools.' Two men designed software that, with very few exceptions, has been taken up as the default metaphor extending from a visualization of analog multi-track tape recording. As Apple computers grew in popularity for music, followed by PCs, the software became more sophisticated, accessible, and widely used.

The expression 'in-the-box' has emerged to describe recording and mixing done entirely within a computer, involving no analog outboard gear beyond the pre-amps used to plug in microphones and other instrument signals. More common in professional studios is the deployment of a mix of computer based DAW equipment combined with outboard gear such as compressors, channel strips and monitoring sections, often based on circuitry from full size consoles. Large analog mixing consoles have maintained an aura of professionalism and have found their way into education institutions due to their usefulness in teaching essential audio engineering concepts.

Code in music production has expanded from being 'burned' into chips on specialized devices such as synths and samplers, to being ubiquitous in tools used for composition, recording, editing, mixing, distribution, and listening. Apart from transducers and converters, almost all analog hardware devices used in music production can be emulated by software. That does not mean that hardware has been totally replaced—not at all—there is still an important market for the haptic, touchable, nostalgic, impressive, and expensive. Turn to a current magazine or website for musicians or audio engineers and analog gear is everywhere. Bennett (2012) explores the range of reasons many recordists choose to use and maintain vintage analog gear. What has changed is that it is no longer as essential. It is important to emphasize that analog and digital technologies have, and continue to, operate together simultaneously, and this goes well beyond the imperative for initial and final analog transduction for recording, then listening purposes (Sterne 2006). Today, equipment that combines digital and analog elements is common; from mixers with analog channel strips that act as USB audio interfaces, to analog synths that allow one to update firmware, save parameters, connect and edit patches and settings with a computer. In addition, some of that hardware is designed to provide input for software (Ableton Live, for example) and contains software embedded in chips as firmware that can be updated. With code crucial to their operation these are clearly examples of codejects.

Disruption narratives focus on commerce, and changes that have occurred when ordinary people were able to harness music in the form of digital data for their own use (Nordgård 2018; Leyshon 2014). Activities around and for music became more computer focused, and therefore code mediated, from ripping CDs, sharing files via the internet, to the subsequent collecting of and listening to mp3 files. The longer history of change, beyond just music encoded as digital data, has been shown here. Central to this has been that code, as mediator and agent has spread and gained ubiquity through instruments, tools of production, and distribution through networks. People writing and using that code as they go about music making and sharing and listening are at the center of these intertwined histories, and the rise of code has seen important changes in skills, roles, and expertise between computing and music.

CHANGING ROLES

Here I map shifts in domains of expertise linked to technology access across two broadly defined groups of people. The first are those involved directly in the technical aspects of professional music production. The second are those who produce music in a more hobby-like, amateur manner. This is a useful starting place, as one of the arguments here is that as music production has become more code-centered, those distinctions become more complicated due to better access to critical tools and changes to industrial infrastructure.

This discussion explores a pivotal transition period, when music recording tools became widely available on ordinary computers. That marks a critical moment where the industrial and commercial balance of music production shifted towards the software/IT sector. This should not be equated with pre- and post-digital. The key pivot is code running on computers in the form of hard disk recording DAWs.

In the pre-DAW studio world, professional audio engineers operated very expensive equipment in custom built spaces at all stages of the recording process. Dominated by large media conglomerates and music labels, budgets were large, and studio personnel relied on tight professional networks of peer recommendation. Computer skills were not required. The exclusivity and limited access to that knowledge, equipment, and space was something desired greatly by those with an interest in music in the amateur realm. Tape based multi-track recording, the dominant technology that preceded digital recording, relied on very expensive, large machines that required specialized maintenance. Even if amateur musicians were capable of using such technology, the cost, the space needed, along with the large mixing consoles they connected to were generally out of reach. In the 1980s, Fostex and Yamaha developed much more affordable multi-track recorders that used standard cassettes, utilizing all four tracks, usually organized as two stereo tape 'sides,' in one direction. Amateurs could then get a taste, although a very reduced one in terms of quality and capability, of multi-track processes and the possibilities it opened up. There were still very sharply demarcated lines between amateur and professional equipment, in terms of cost, space needed, maintenance needs, and any associated skills required. Indeed, professional audio producers were (and still are) known as audio 'engineers,' a title that carries professional status usually conferred on degree graduates accredited by professional bodies. This is not the case with those involved in music.

The title engineer for audio recording professionals stems from a time where electrical and electronic engineering were skills used on a daily basis. Engineers in the studio recording environment were fixing, developing, modifying, and using the equipment they were using to record. Although many modern engineers might be adept at soldering, detailed knowledge of the workings of the equipment and how to customize and repair it is not as important as it was for an older generation working primarily in the analog domain.[2] From around 2000, as hard disk recording overtook stand-alone devices like the ADAT, audio engineers became computer users. What we see with the rise of DAWs is that the computer infrastructure to run professional software in studios was essentially the same as that present in homes and offices.

Within a few years, computers which were increasingly common in offices and homes brought the experience of multi-track recording to a much wider population. All that was required was software, and an appropriate audio interface. A growing number of people had the opportunity to dip into audio engineering, with access to similar tools or at least digital versions of them. In the late 1990s I worked at the University of Papua New Guinea teaching music, and although we had a large format analog console that had been donated by the Japanese government some years before, along with a 2-inch tape machine, access was strictly in the hands of a few trusted colleagues; I didn't even bother asking to use it, in fact. At the time, I recall seeing in a music magazine an advertisement for the music software *Cubase* (for Windows 95, I believe) and ordered it, fascinated by the potential of what was described as "Virtual Studio Technology" to provide me with a personal multi-track experience.

Connections in skills and knowledge that had existed between audio engineers and their specialized equipment changed. Audio engineers needed to become computer users. Most people adapted quickly, but often there was a wide disparity between a specialized body of knowledge on recording, microphone choice, placement, pre-amp selection, outboard gear use, large format console use, and the use of software. Many audio engineers develop acute listening skills, and may use these strategically to assert their status in the field and manipulate the psychology of their clients around sound quality. I remember, for example, being told by a highly regarded audio engineer as I discussed some recordings we were sending him to mix that the DAW we were using sounded a lot better than another more commonly used DAW when tracks were exported for mixing. He had worked with high profile classical and popular music artists internationally stretching back for decades, and regularly contributed articles to recording magazines. I felt I was in no position of authority from an industry perspective to argue that I felt this was unlikely, and let it slide. I had a similar experience some years earlier with a mastering engineer, who also praised the particular DAW we were using (not ProTools, I should add) because of its alleged sound.

In these cases, the engineers were most likely making me feel better about the slightly non-standard choice of DAW the institution I worked for had chosen (Nuendo—a version of Cubase), and I did not upset the hierarchy of expertise by asking them to explain their views, knowing that it was highly likely their understanding of digital principles and code was scant. Knowledge in the analog domain does not automatically translate to the digital. Recounting these stories to friends of mine with electronic and software engineering degrees who design and build digital systems has confirmed this.

The specialized nature of audio equipment and recording processes over several decades led to a close relationship in the domains of knowledge between users of equipment and its designers and builders, even though this might have been as simple as an understanding of basic electronic circuits and an ability to solder. As specialized software running on generic hardware entered the tool chain in recording, audio engineers became software users rather than software fixers, or designers. Studio engineers, as this process occurred, became highly adept users of computers, but few were able to mix the detailed software engineering skills required with the creative skills and networks of musicians and reputations that was central to the functioning of the music industries. The relatively rapid shift in knowledge required perhaps explains the various digital myths and doubtful opinions of some experts in the analog domain as just described.

Audio professionals had to transfer their existing domain knowledge across to a new device and operating interface. That, in itself as a process was by no means new. Studio professionals have moved from tape in various formats, to ADAT, and had used other digital equipment. What was new was that amateurs increasingly had those same basic tools (computers) along with the same essential skills to use them. A certain exclusivity around access to once expensive equipment in dedicated spaces changed. As a result, there was a demand for the audio engineering knowledge and skills. The internet expanded information sharing so that the domain knowledge was no longer spread in a craft-like manner from professional to apprentice.

Income and opportunities for professional music producers dropped with the decimation of major label recording budgets and the associated large dedicated recording studio scene. At the same time as this there was extraordinary growth in audio education courses, teaching a generation of enthusiastic, optimistic musicians, and recordists the range of skills that are needed for modern recording. That most of these graduates end up recording at home or in small project studios making music from which they will gain very little income suggests the selling of dreams and exploitation of an education market more than anything, and the sustainability of this situation is questionable. Never have so many ex-professional audio engineers moved into teaching institutions to teach so many students skills from which they are unlikely to earn an income. Longer term resident music academics, myself included, have been complicit in this too, of course, creating courses in digital production and audio engineering without providing adequate analysis of the state of employment in creative industries. There are notable exceptions to this—Real Industry (https://realindustry.org/)—as perhaps the most innovative and inspiring example, connecting music tech industries (often software based) with university students.

This state of affairs benefits the IT industry relying as it does on large numbers of content providers, providing material for essentially no cost to the software companies in the business ultimately of advertising.

TRANSECTORIAL INNOVATION

Music commerce is more connected to the computing industry than any other. Music and the computing industries are not parallel phenomena. They are bound together, and that is likely to continue for some time. This merging has involved the acquisition of different skills—operating computers, for example—and shifts in knowledge. This leads to one of the important aspects of a code musicology which is that significant concerns in the field of computing will matter for music, and our musicology will need to move these concepts more to the center of analytical focus.

One way of thinking about this has been through the idea of *transectorial innovation*, a term coined from economics describing shifts in power, activity, relationships and commerce when one industrial sector moves in on another (Piatier 1988). For the purposes here, that is largely the IT sector moving in on the music sector (Sterne 2012, 203), often called the music industry, but actually a more fragmented, complex aggregation, better known as the music industries (Williamson and Cloonan 2007) or simply seen as part of a complex mix (Sterne 2014a). As Morris (2015) points out, in relation to music: "Transectorial innovation has made music and computing interdependent and conflicted bedfellows" (21).

This has a longer history, perhaps most clearly demonstrated by contradictions within a corporation like Sony, when the electronics division of the company built a CD player that could play mp3 files from a CD: "While Sony Music sought to stop the growing swarm of MP3s, Sony Electronics either had to capitalize on it or be left out of the market. The conflict inside Sony encapsulated the conflict across industries" (Sterne 2012, 208).

If transectorial innovation describes incremental processes contributing to change, then another term—perhaps sectorial transformation—needs to be applied once the new sector has become dominant. This is certainly the case for recorded music in the Global North, and is becoming the case more globally. Music commerce is IT commerce; music industries are software industries.

Companies such as Google, Facebook, and Apple, with software at the core of their business models, are the main players in recent transectorial innovation in music industries. The recording commodity that was once central to music industries has changed to something that is at the center of the new sector—data. Software companies have no interest in creating and selling physical incarnations of fundamentally digital phenomena. Instead, income generation has shifted to data surrounding digital music activity that can be used for advertising purposes.

Streaming services are a form of software solution in that the user is offered convenience—a huge library to choose from—for a subscription fee or being subject to advertising, but having no access to the musical digital object for use in other applications. Music moves to being more of a service than a collection of files on a device under such conditions (Nag 2018). The exchange of our metadata for online services such as YouTube, as well as the opportunity to have ads played to us are fundamental approaches that make sense in a vast network with billions of small transactions in the form of viewing activities by individual users. These service providers collect and store information about what we listen to, when, and how often. This aspect of data collection is the key difference. Social media sites and apps such as YouTube, Facebook, and WhatsApp are also commonly used for listening to music, and again, the apparent freedom in terms of both cost and rights comes at a price. As internet security expert Bruce Schneier has pointed out:

> Surveillance is the business model of the internet. Everyone is under constant surveillance by many companies, ranging from social networks like Facebook to cellphone providers. This data is collected, compiled, analyzed, and used to try to sell us stuff. Personalized advertising is how these companies make money, and is why so much of the internet is free to users. We're the product, not the customer. (Mineo 2017)

So, for music, transectorial innovation ultimately means different people are making money by treating the same fundamental content (recorded music) as a conduit to collect different commodities—data.

As software and music continue to intertwine, the politics of professional power swing towards those creating the code. This happened within computing also, with Ensmenger (2010, 2003) examining shifts in power within organizations and businesses as the role of computer programmer developed from the 1950s onwards. Managers, while relying on the work of programmers, often did not understand the specifics of what they actually did. Early on, programming was regarded as craft-like, and for quite a while they were thought of as being somewhere between technical staff and engineers. For many years they were not regarded as professionals. Programming is now of course a respected discipline of engineering (software engineering) and recognized area of scientific research (computer science). Code and power are clearly linked today. Code dominates the core operations of some of the largest corporations of the 21st century. The power wielded by Google and Facebook, companies with code as their main asset, is widely recognized, if not feared even. As this kind of transectorial change occurs in music, shifts in power lead to some important questions.

CODING AND DIVERSITY

Throughout the first part of the 21st century, the life around code—so the people who have made it in contexts where it has had the most effect—are from remarkably narrow fields of life and associated experiences; usually white, male, Global North. While there are software developers all over the world, the most widespread applications are created in technology centers such as Silicon Valley mainly by men with a relatively narrow range of backgrounds and musical experience. These people largely create the software that has an increasingly significant effect on the world's music making, recording, sharing, listening, and discussing. There is an obvious tension between the diversity of people making music globally, and that of the bulk of people creating music software.

This is part of a broader set of problems for software development. As Morris and Elkins (2015) point out: "There's been little change in the developer profile as well, which remains overwhelmingly male (94%) and American (54%)" (74). Software developed in such an environment, unsurprisingly, can build in discrimination. Consider the "AI white guy problem" (Crawford 2016) where "Sexism, racism and other forms of discrimination are being built into the machine-learning algorithms that underlie the technology behind many "intelligent" systems that shape how we are categorized and advertised to." As the targeting of advertising becomes an important part of business models for companies like Google and Facebook, discrimination is seen there as well; a recent example being women not being shown online ads for highly paid jobs (Spice 2015).

Witness the trouble some people in the IT sector are having coming to terms with changes as attitudes towards diversity and equality impact working lives. As I write, a Google employee has been fired for propounding sexist views on women engineers, and the topic of rampant sexism in Silicon Valley has re-surfaced (Tiku 2017). These problems are intensified in places where sexism is more entrenched (see, for example, Ajiboye [2017]). Coleman (2013), in an in-depth ethnography of coding culture also shows this with the white, male, Global North makeup of the community building and maintaining the Debian distribution of Linux. Music production, and many other aspects of music industries have been male-dominated and sexist as detailed by Brooks et al. (2021). What might the consequences be for musical diversity and balance from the encoding of particular contexts and values? What might a study from the perspective of code reveal about the dangers of obscurity, bias, and so on specifically in regard to musical practice? It is to a series of such code-centered topics that the following chapters now turn.

NOTES

1. The term porting means transferring software to a different operating system, usually involving re-writing and re-organization of certain parts of the codebase.

2. See Kealy (1979) and Horning (2004) for more on the history and changing skills of audio engineers.

Chapter Three

Coding Constraints

Increasingly involved in various aspects of music, code provides constraints and limits on sonic results and associated musical activities. This chapter examines what these constraints look like in their guise as abstractions. Code also allows, encourages, even inspires musical possibilities. This aspect is explored through the idea of affordances. The effects of these constraints and affordances is then examined.

Music technology is a highly social phenomena, from the building process, to marketing, and usage. Drawing on Hutchby (2001) the idea of affordances is a useful way to think about how music technology is part of musical and social practice. In particular, it can help map a spectrum of views of technology ranging from hard determinist positions to those of unbounded human agency. All forms of technology have limitations. Some things are possible, others are not; some things are easier to implement than others, so the idea of constraints is useful here. Magnusson (2006) and D'Errico (2016) use the phrase "affordances and constraints" which serves as a useful frame to think about the kind of limitations and possibilities that code provides. D'Errico (2016), Strachan (2017), and others use these ideas to explore how people create music with particular software, and how its design influences music. Their focus here is on user interfaces, the GUI controls, underlying metaphors, and resulting workflows. Interfaces are simply the visual result of running code, of course, so here my purpose is to move beyond the interface, into an examination of deeper structures in code that afford and constrain.

Music software, with perhaps only a few exceptions targeted at specialists, has largely developed to create the sort of popular music common in the Global North, with an Anglophone bias. Following Greene (2005, 6) some simple examples illustrate how this may end up structuring music. When one opens a sequencer or DAW application for the first time in almost any of the numerous main applications, the tempo is set around 120bpm and there is a time signature of 4/4. While both parameters are easily adjustable, there is a default assumption about structure as a starting point. A virtual piano keyboard is often available, in turn assuming Western equal tempered tuning, along with specific notions of key, scales, notation and so on. This has been a phenomenon of the hardwired, analogue world as well, as Greene (2005) points out:

> By design, some sound qualities and techniques are easier to produce and others more difficult. As a result, in many places the advent of western sound-engineering technologies has reinforced trends toward western equal-tempered scales with discrete pitches. Thus as western sound technologies are drawn into music making around the world, their hardwirings begin to structure local musical practices in certain ways, imposing their own musical logics onto the societies that adopt them. Hardwirings constitute a (sometimes subsonic) vehicle of control in the world's musical praxis, and technological musicking—perhaps more so that traditional musicking—becomes a struggle that engages with the translocal. (6)

And, related to the spread of sound technologies, but again in the hardwired world: "As sound technologies are increasingly consumed in the non-western world, it remains to be seen to what extent future hardware models will better reflect the expressive needs of musicians operating outside the creative limitations of current western-designed technologies" (6).

With the increasing prominence of software-based sound technologies, are similar concerns present? Given that many software interfaces feature skeuomorphs of analog devices such as those in commercial studios in the West, this would seem likely. They bring with them particular contexts, aesthetic values, practices, and relationships. As described earlier though, interfaces themselves are instances of running code. Code is put together with particular structures in mind, and certain libraries and associated technologies are deliberately chosen. How do affordances emerge in this environment? What constraints are evident as a result of the way digital devices such as computers are built? How are layers of code as examples of formal materiality designed based on practical workarounds to elements that percolate through from the forensic materiality of digital hardware? What might this present for new musical possibilities? How does latency, for example, act as a constraint, and perhaps afford certain kinds of processes and actions over others?

I examine three main areas in some detail. The first is time, and how to reconcile musical time with how computers operate. This is a good example of how insights gleaned from thinking beyond the interface, into the code that creates it, can be useful. I then look at languages that have been developed to compose and create music, and specifically what they offer for new ideas as to what music might be able to become. Finally, I explore particular code libraries, looking at the time that goes into making them, the politics and processes in the things that get implemented, and again, what that might mean for music in the future.

DIGITAL TIME, MUSICAL TIME

Music technology frequently needs to organize sound in time. There are important differences between analog and digital domains as to the nature and complexity of such processes. Particularly in code driven environments, the way hardware and low-level software has been designed offers challenges for organizing sounds to unfold in ways that make sense to people. People writing code negotiate constraints from digital hardware through a combination of software layers and associated abstractions. This in turn affords the potential for musical forms that play with the resultant possibilities. Strachan (2017) and Bell (2018) among others make the strong argument that digital tools such as DAWs end up shaping music in distinct ways as a result of the ease with which manipulation can occur in musical time. Styles that come to life through cutting, looping, combining and re-combining, principally in the time domain, are used as examples.

Both music and running code occur as sequences of events in time. While music organizes sound in time, running code organizes machine instructions in time. The timescales over which both unfold overlap. This provides a useful analytical conduit to consider how the mediation of music by code affords changes in music, and also how the kinds of changes that are valued in music shape approaches to the nature of code and coding. It is useful to compare the timescales and the manner in which regular events are scheduled and occur.

Let us consider a common, simple recording scenario. A person sings into a microphone, the sound of which we wish to modify with a filter, before recording it. Once the sound of the voice has been converted to a continuous electrical signal and amplified appropriately, it is fed into a series of electronic components in a circuit that modifies that signal. One of the simplest such circuits is that of a high pass filter, designed to allow frequencies above a certain cut-off frequency to pass unaltered, while attenuating those below. This consists of a capacitor and a resistor in series. Due to the way in which a capacitor operates, lower frequencies applied to the input do not pass through, while higher ones do. The cutoff frequency is determined here by the type and specifications of the components used. As our continuously changing signal is applied to the input, a modified version with different frequency content appears at the output. As this occurs at close to the speed of light, from a human perspective it is essentially instant.

The digital version of this is more complicated. The continuously changing voltage of the signal created by our microphone is converted at a certain rate into a series of numbers, known as samples. We now have what is known as a *discrete* signal. The digital version of our filter is *discretized* as an equation that operates on these samples sequentially and, in this case at least, along with one or more preceding it. This is all being carried out by code, which consists of a series of instructions held in computer memory that are executed in a particular sequence. The way these are timed involves the use of the CPU (Central Processing Unit) clock.[1] The CPU, which is the main control center of a computer has its timing controlled by an oscillator. This generates a fixed frequency sine wave which is then converted to a square wave pulse to represent the 0 and 1 states at the core of our digital computing. Today CPUs run in billions of cycles per second (5 gigahertz was about the fastest at the time of writing). Instructions throughout the layers of firmware and software are then scheduled and run at varying points in the clock signal, depending on how many cycles, and therefore how long they take to run. Some operations need to wait for others, and signals are sent between layers and instruction aggregates to coordinate this.

That modified signal is then converted back to an analog electrical one. For audio to be perceived once its digital representation has been processed digitally, audio samples are sent to a buffer, which serves as a holding place for sequential data. This is then converted into an analog signal again by a Digital to Audio Converter (DAC). That buffer holds a number of amplitude points at a particular sample rate, so the buffer size relates to time as a result of that sample rate relationship. If the sample rate is 44100Hz, and the buffer holds 44100 samples, then the buffer represents a time length of 1 second. On the digital side, the software needs to fill that buffer at least every second, otherwise there is nothing to convert to analog, and a glitch occurs. The rate at which this buffer needs to be filled provides a fixed delay, known as latency. The term *realtime* has been coined, and is shared with other time critical fields, to describe systems that are designed to reliably keep the buffers filled within an appropriate time period for human perception.

Navigating this low-level architecture with more human scales and concepts of musical time is difficult. Paul Davis, the main developer of the open-source DAW Ardour, points this out after a lengthy discussion of problems converting between what he describes as musical time (so a particular position in relation to a time signature with a certain tempo) and audio time (the numerical representation of a point in time):

> It is incredible how much of a DAW is really about time—representing it, manipulating it, storing it—and so nutempo has involved changes to 10's of thousands of lines of code. So many user operations are fundamentally about changing time values in some way—dragging things, stretching things, deleting

things, trimming etc.—and every single one of these will need to be carefully evaluated in a whole series of thoroughly designed tests to check that I have not broken them. (Randolph 2018)

He points out how the start of a note can possibly be missed if rounding errors accumulate while converting back and forth between musical and audio time. Notes can move, be missed, as ultimately code involves decisions involving numerical comparisons. The human perception of time, and indeed analog representations of it, are continuous so when music is represented numerically, things get complicated and there is a negotiation between machine requirements, calculations, and how abstractions get coded.

Although computation for audio processing in modern systems can take place well within the time constraints that become important for human comprehension of time, the increasing number of layers creates challenges, and developers are left to rely on solid architecture being designed into the particular operating system being used. There are limits, as Wang, Cook, and Salazar (2015) point out: "In practice, real-time audio will remain robust up to the limit imposed by computing speed, after which audio will experience glitches and interruptions—as is the case for any real-time synthesis system" (16).

In an interview with Glenn Dickins, a DSP software engineer working for Dolby on realtime audio, he pointed out that it seemed to him to be harder to get glitch-free realtime audio now than in 1997, when he worked on a system that operated with just three samples of latency in and out. He stated that there are very few operating system configurations he can now rely on for glitch-free audio. He suggested that visual aspects were now getting higher priority than audio, giving an example of a phone app where 90 percent of the processing time is spent updating pixels on a representation of a guitar fretboard leaving little for the actual sound (interview, June 15, 2018).

If latency as a result of poor audio performance is longer than 10ms or so, a distinct echo or delay effect is heard, and as it lengthens, becomes increasingly noticeable and irritating. While most computer systems and iOS devices are capable of keeping that latency at or around this amount, latencies on the most common computer systems globally—Android—vary wildly, from an acceptable 20ms or so to 200ms and longer. To make it worse, these times in the Android environment on a single device can vary greatly, so there is no consistency to enable adjustments to be made. A company built on licensing software to mitigate against these constraints, Superpowered, provide a list of these latency figures. They offer the following take on the impacts that the ridiculously poor latency performance of Android has:

> Music instruments apps, audio effect apps: musicians cannot play together on stage, as the performer using an Android device will be a half beat behind the others. It's not even usable for practicing.

DJs can not perform beat-matching, as their pre-listening signal in their headphones is far behind the master signal playing for the audience. Applying effects like a loop roll or echo is very hard too.

Games: sound effects, such as explosions or gun sounds lag behind by a few frames. Game audio is then "detached" from visuals, making for poor user-experience, preventing immersive gaming experiences.

VOIP apps, such as Skype: if both users are using a high latency Android phone, the overall audio latency is higher than the network latency. In other words, it takes more time for audio to "flow" through Android, than data packets to be transferred between continents.

Virtual reality (VR): when the viewer turns his head, the audio "follows" too late, destroying the 3D audio experience. Check the Paul McCartney Google Cardboard app for an example. Google is on the verge of leaving billions in revenue in VR opportunities for Apple. (Superpowered 2016)

Quite clearly, Android was not originally designed with the needs of music recording and production in mind. What about situations where music was firmly at the center of design decisions? Negotiating differences between human perceptions of time and the way machines organize instructions reveal interesting avenues for discussion. Recently, in trying out a programming language for making music, ChucK, I came across the keyword "now" and was intrigued that such a commonly invoked term in daily life had a central role in organizing time within the environment. According to the documentation, here are some of the properties of now:

TEXTBOX 3.1: PROPERTIES OF "NOW" (CHUCK, N.D)

Some properties of now include:

now holds the current ChucK time (when read).

modifying now has the side effects of:

advancing time (see below);

suspending the current process (called shred) until the desired time is reached - allowing other shreds and audio synthesis to compute;

the value of now only changes when it is explicitly modified.

Largely designed by computer music expert Ge Wang, with contributions from others in the field, this represents a highly sophisticated understanding of the importance of managing and navigating time for making music, not just listening to recordings. Here are some examples of "now" in use (again, from the documentation):

> **TEXTBOX 3.2: EXAMPLES OF USE OF "NOW"**
>
> ```
> // compute value that represents "5 seconds from now"
> now + 5::second => time later;
>
> // while we are not at later yet...
> while( now < later )
> {
>     // print out value of now
>     <<< now >>>;
>
>     // advance time by 1 second
>     1::second => now;
> }
> ```

The very idea of asking if now is before (less than) later, and the concept of being able to advance time by one second is fascinating in giving programmers conceptual controls not available in our analog modes of perception and agency: "ChucK defines the notion of a strongly timed audio programming language, comprising a versatile time-based programming model that allows programmers to flexibly and precisely control the flow of time in code and use the keyword now as a time-aware control construct" (10, abstract).

The notion of *now* is, under some consideration, not as simple as it first seems. When I am playing a musical instrument, or listening to music, I have an awareness of sounds immediately past; indeed to make sense of sound in a musical context (or a language context) is to place it in context with that which has just recently occurred. Human hearing and the ability to perceive closely arriving sounds in time as being single events, echos, or separate auditory events occurs over a range up to around 100ms. It therefore seems reasonable in musical terms at least to think of now as a slightly flexible window of time somewhere between where we differentiate an echo from repetition of a fast note that we can track while playing or listening (so say a

16th note at 180bpm—so less than 100ms). The main point here is that code abstractions to deal with digital environments reveal that apparently simple concepts like *now*, as an example, are not nearly as straightforward as they might at first seem. People writing code to generate music spend a great deal of time thinking about, abstracting and implementing ways of organizing time so that sound can be generated in ways that make sense to humans. As Wang states "It is our hope that ChucK provides a unique way of working with and thinking about time—and its variety of interactions with sound and music" (28). In a series of artist statements at the end of Wang's chapter Wang (2007), Carsten Nicolai expresses how his "main focus then was, and now still is primarily oriented towards the question of how time is perceived through sound" (83). Ultimately this can effect the music created from such tools and, as Wang, Cook, and Salazar (2015) point out: "A programming language cannot help but shape the way we think about solving particular problems" (27) and how:

> Time is intimately connected with sound and is central to how audio and music programs are created and reasoned about. This may seem like an obvious point—as sound and music are intrinsically time-based phenomena—yet we feel that control over time in programming languages is underrepresented (or sometimes over-abstracted). Low-level languages such as C/C++ and Java have no inherent notion of time but allow custom data types to represent time, which can be cumbersome to implement and to use. High-level computer music languages tend to abstract time too much. (10)

Perhaps most significantly, there is always some period over which it is a trivial computing task to be able to freely re-order audio samples in time, or amplitude, or both. Analog audio processing is geared towards processing in sequence, and while some re-ordering of audio is possible, the potential for complete re-ordering like this is much harder. In the digital domain, there is processing time available to adjust linear audio time, radically if desired, and to re-combine it at will. From the computing processing time perspective of the CPU, there are millions of instruction cycles available to take a chunk of sample data and process it before being sent to the buffer.

PROGRAMMING LANGUAGES FOR MUSIC

While it is a given that at some level programmers must navigate design around the quirks of the forensic materiality of digital hardware, at higher levels of code design in the formal material domain, we see music specific languages, through to code libraries that do their best to massage languages not so designed to deal with music more efficiently. Composers saw opportunities for composition and devised ways of coding music from the earliest days of computing. For many years, this activity was confined to universities and research centers where the large, unwieldy, expensive machines requiring specialist support resided. The history of this, and the contribution to Western art music is well documented (Manning 2004; Chadabe 1997). That tradition continues today as a field widely recognized as computer music, associated journals, groups and conferences.[2]

This trajectory of music and computing involves the creation of specifically focused music programming languages, interfaces, and environments such as PureData and Max/MSP. Forward thinking, and forging deep connections between technical complexity and artistic expression, this field has over half a century history of providing materials, insights, and philosophical musings that the world of more mainstream music production has been slow to harness. Attempts from this field to engage with more everyday music making practices has been a more active pursuit, from musical activities as part of the OLPC project using CSound, to projects at research centers such as IRCAM, CNMAT and CCRMA. The work of Ge Wang, in particular, has had wide reach through smartphone apps, other software, and most recently, a thoroughly engaging, future focused, expansive book on design with musical examples as case studies (Wang 2018).

Programming languages with text-based interfaces (i.e., one codes them directly) extend from what Wang (2007) describes as the "MUSIC N" family, starting with Max Mathews' MUSIC in 1957 (58). Due to the limitations of early computers, code would be written, then compiled and run to produce output. As computers increased in power, higher level languages appeared, often interpreted, so that code can be written and rendered to audio on the fly.

There are two important abstractions that these early languages set up. The first is the idea of abstracting instruments (or orchestra) from scores (lists of notes). A good example of this is the language Csound. A simple example provided by the getting started web page shows Csound statements separated by the "tags" in brackets (<>) divided into an instrument and score section:

> **TEXTBOX 3.3: EXAMPLE OF CSOUND CODE (CSOUND, N.D.)**
>
> ```
> <CsoundSynthesizer>
> <CsInstruments>
>
> instr 1
> aOut vco2 1, p4
> out aOut
> endin
>
> </CsInstruments>
> <CsScore>
> i1 0 1 100
> i1 1 1 200
> i1 2 1 300
> </CsScore>
> </CsoundSynthesizer>
> ```

Written by Barry Vercoe at MIT and released in 1986, it is part of the MUSIC-N lineage, and shows how traditional, obvious composition approaches and concepts such as orchestra and score were used as models for new music. Longevity is built into these languages and tools through being open source. This provides a potential lifespan for backwards and forwards compatibility that proprietary systems have completely failed to achieve: "One of the main principles in Csound development is to guarantee backwards compatibility. You can still render a Csound source file from 1986 on the latest Csound release, and you should be able to render a file written today with the latest Csound in 2036" (Csound, n.d.b).

The second important abstraction is separating rates that render audio to a DAC (audio rate) from those that control various parameters (control rate). The control rates have generally been much slower than the audio rate, and this helps with managing computing resources. Part of the thinking behind this is that there is no need to adjust gain, say, at the same rate as rendering audio because people cannot and for musical purposes do not need to discern such fine-grained time domain differences. This is yet another example where a code focused analysis brings out the extent to which designers, programmers, composers, and musicians are forced to grapple with reconciling notions of computer time, human perceptions of time, and available computing power.

If managing time for music demonstrates compromises that need to be made for performance, there are examples where structures that have become central to computing have found useful applications in music. SuperCollider, for example, is a language built on a server and client model, with a protocol known as 'Open Sound Control' (OSC) communicating between client and server. Coinciding with increased capabilities in the realtime rendering of audio, languages like this specifically cater for on the fly programming, something to be discussed in more detail in the next chapter under "live coding." One front end, known as *Tidal*, built using the functional programming language Haskell, makes it very easy for a coder to sequence samples or other sounds within a cycle. As Wang, Cook, and Salazar (2015, 13) point out, SuperCollider and some other languages, like ChucK, have removed the distinction between orchestra and score. This can be seen as another example of how structures from the computing realm such as client and server models interact with a tradition of music languages that have built on established pre-digital concepts from musical composition.

The way these languages are designed means they can be used as music "engines" or backends for applications with graphical and other interfaces. Different capabilities of these languages offer affordances by making some things easier to implement, while providing constraints. New musical forms have emerged from these affordances and constraints. Nick Collins, for examples describes his "corposition" (Collins 2017):

> A two-minute-long 16-channel electroacoustic tape piece was first premiered in June 2015, using a provisional 1,000-work subset of the final corpus. A progression from 1950 to 1999 at one second per year was formed from short extracts of corpus pieces; the unequal holdings over the chronology led to different densities of material around the 16 channels. After a silence for reflection, the piece regressed in time the opposite way, this time with works overlapping each other as they survived for a few seconds following spatial arcs through the room. Finally, after another pause, the piece returned to 1999, this time traveling 50 years in one second. (48)

Corposition is "a portmanteau of "corpus" and "composition" indicating musical works that exploit a large collection of music files" (47) The ease with which digitized audio can be manipulated in a granular manner invites such experimentation and new forms as (Collins 2017) states: "Corposition gives an explicit route for a corposer to reveal a relationship with the past. Successive layers of precedent and influence can be peeled back as historic time becomes a compositional parameter, or alternative nonchronological routes can be explored based on extracted audio features and associated metadata" (48).

Collins describes his piece as being at the opposite end of the spectrum of Trevor Wishart's piece *Imago* (2002) "which creates a 25-minute work from a single clink of wine glasses; here a week of audio is used to render a highly time-compressed output" (48)

MUSIC CODE LIBRARIES

While these music specific languages have offered great opportunities for new musics and experimentation, more mainstream digital music production involves using applications whose coding has relied on massaging mainstream computer languages (such as C++ and Java) to musical purposes. Applications are built using a number of code libraries and application programming interfaces (APIs), which provide programmers with easier, time saving ways of carrying out frequently required functions.

As an example, many developers writing music programs need to be able to read and write audio files. Rather than everyone having to write their own code individually to do this, people choose existing libraries. One such widely used example is the *libsndfile* library written by Erik de Castro Lopo (Libsndfile, n.d.). A programmer simply imports the library into their own project, and can open a file with a few lines of code. The *libsndfile* library then takes care of the multitude of possibilities and problems that would otherwise take the programmer hundreds, if not thousands, of lines of code. Libraries provide affordances and constraints and the choice of which to use can have long lasting effects on a program. Choosing a less sophisticated, or unreliably maintained library over *libsndfile*, for example, might mean certain file types would be unreadable, bugs would remain unfixed, and some operations might not be possible at all. This section maps out a series of examples of constraints and affordances in music libraries by starting at the top of representative of the application code stack—user interface elements—before working down through lower code layers.

Limitations from designs in user interface have their roots in code. Individual elements of an interface, such as check-boxes and buttons are aggregations of code known as functions, or better objects and associated methods. Berry (2016, 9), in setting out a philosophy of software points out how reading code exposes assumptions and limits possibilities. An electronic voter system is examined to provide an example (116). The code Berry analyses reveals that the choice of a particular user interface element—in this case a radio box which only allows specific preset choices—means that it is impossible for voters to make a protest vote, as would be possible with a paper-based system. Further, quite specific assumptions and biases can be seen in comments, variable names, method names, even library names. Again, with the voter system, Berry points out how a programmer specifically refers to voters as "he" in the source code. Nakamura (2002) explores similar matters in a chapter on "menu-driven identities" where limited choices in interface design are discussed. It is important to note here that interface elements are usually provided by code libraries.

In addition to gender assumptions, decisions are made from particular understandings and experiences of musical structure and context. As an example, the pioneering music library developed for NeXT computers, the MusicKit, uses terms such as "orchestra" to describe particular object oriented classes. Object oriented programming relies on the programmer conceptualizing solutions based on a series of abstractions that map to existing objects and concepts. Here are some notes in the documentation about the overall design of the library:

> Music is represented in a three-level hierarchy. A Score represents a section of musical material and contains Parts. A Part is analogous to an instrumental part in an orchestral score and corresponds to a rendering in a particular manner. It contains a sorted list of Notes, each representing an event with a particular onset time. (MusicKitOverview.rtf in MusicKit 2009)

There is also the notion of a performance, orchestra, and conductor in the MusicKit. The architecture of such a library has been carefully thought about and designed with application developers in mind:

> The Music Kit suggests a variety of exciting applications. Its vitality will be determined by the imagination of the software developers who build on its foundation. We feel that the power of the concepts on which it is based, such as the abstraction of performance, the extensibility of the Note, and the modular approach to synthesis, is capable of meeting the needs of a wide variety of application developers. (MusicKitOverview.rtf in MusicKit 2009)

Delving further into library classes and APIs to see how concepts have been implemented and connected offers analytical insight into the delimiting effects software using those libraries is likely to encounter. The benefits of an open source library like this are that we have the opportunity to take this code, and modify it to address any criticisms we might have. While such libraries might well be ideally suited to certain types of music and associated processes and activities, the effects are likely to be more felt when attempting to accommodate more diverse contexts. Libraries can be thought of as operating at a number of levels. A library like this is designed for application developers to be able to implement high level ideas such as a DAW or music notation program. These libraries then use other libraries, thought of being at a lower level, to implement their needs, and so on. It is layers of libraries all the way down, really. Determining which libraries to look at, and in what sort of detail is a critical part of a code focused musicology, and the following examples map out some examples and guiding principles.

The examples I have chosen provide musical and sound capabilities in web browsers. This is for a number of reasons. There has been a trend over the last couple of decades for common tasks to be carried out in browsers—word processing, for example. While video editing and music production might be difficult problems in this space due to the bandwidth and intensive processing required, there are recent developments that make this all the more possible and likely. Another reason speaks to power through the sorts of business models dominated by the IT sector, driven by Google and others deriving income from advertising. If people spend more time in a browser, more data can be collected and more advertisements can be broadcast.

The lowest level library I describe is Web Audio, accessed through an Application Programming Interface (API) in Javascript. To have these run in a variety of mainstream browsers, these APIs need to be standardized. There is a centralized organization known as the "W3C" that establishes such standards for the web and associated browsers: "The World Wide Web Consortium (W3C) is an international community where Member organizations, a full-time staff, and the public work together to develop Web standards" (W3C, n.d.).

The standards are open and can be examined. Browser developers then implement these standards and they have large effects globally. Two big players in music currently, Google and Apple, develop their own internet browsers; Apple has Safari, and Google has Chrome, which also provides code for the open-source Chromium. Digging further into these layers, the Web Audio API forms part of the Javascript engine implemented by different browsers.

We are not able to simply peruse the source code for proprietary browsers such as Safari (developed by Apple), but looking at the browser implementation charts for Web Audio shows how extensive the spec is (Mozilla, n.d.). Browsers are often largely written in C++. While digging in to the implementation of the Web Audio spec in the open source browser Firefox, I perused the code at the repository where these C++ files are located (Webaudio, n.d.). I then noticed a directory which contains code written by people at Google, and that is used in Google's implementation of the Web Audio spec.

The code for Chromium (the open-source version of Google's Chrome) at another repository shows their version (Chromium, n.d.). So from this, the spec from the two browsers is based on the same code. If a compressor is applied in the audio chain, then the ultimate code that deals with specific audio buffers and changes their dynamic range is essentially shared. Digging a bit deeper, there are differences, however. Firefox developers had fixed a bug in the Compressor code avoiding a divide by zero error, for example.

The audio working group of W3C have devised some potential scenarios for which a Web Audio standard might be able to address. The constitution of the group that put these cases together in 2013 consist of people from browser developers (Mozilla, Opera, Apple, Google, Microsoft), academia/research, invited experts, broadcasting (BBC), Intel, and AI software company Nuance (WebAudio 2013). Suggested use cases include:

1. Video chat application
2. 3D game with music and convincing sound effects
3. Online music production tool
4. Online radio broadcast
5. Music creation environment with sampled instruments
6. Connected DJ booth
7. Playful sonification of user interfaces
8. Podcast on a flight
9. Short film with director's commentary and audio description
10. Web-based guitar practice service
11. User control of audio

Ultimately, audio becomes a fundamental part of the web browser architecture, rather than an afterthought or added extra provided by third-party plugins:

> Audio on the web has been fairly primitive up to this point and until very recently has had to be delivered through plugins such as Flash and QuickTime. The introduction of the audio element in HTML5 is very important, allowing for basic streaming audio playback. But, it is not powerful enough to handle more complex audio applications. For sophisticated web-based games or interactive applications, another solution is required. It is a goal of this specification to include the capabilities found in modern game audio engines as well as some of the mixing, processing, and filtering tasks that are found in modern desktop audio production applications.
>
> The APIs have been designed with a wide variety of use cases in mind. Ideally, it should be able to support any use case which could reasonably be implemented with an optimized C++ engine controlled via script and run in a browser. That said, modern desktop audio software can have very advanced capabilities, some of which would be difficult or impossible to build with this system. Apple's Logic Audio is one such application which has support for external MIDI controllers, arbitrary plugin audio effects and synthesizers, highly optimized direct-to-disk audio file reading/writing, tightly integrated time-stretching, and so on. Nevertheless, the proposed system will be quite capable of supporting a large range of reasonably complex games and interactive applications, including musical ones. And it can be a very good complement

to the more advanced graphics features offered by WebGL. The API has been designed so that more advanced capabilities can be added at a later time. (WebAudio, 2021a)

The use case for music production has quite high requirements but essentially includes many of the capabilities using audio clips and files of a stand-alone DAW (WebAudio 2013). Interestingly, although perhaps unsurprisingly given that such possibilities are built into the fundamental design, a number of such applications exist already as online DAWs with various business models (most subscription based) to create music in a Web Audio capable browser. The essential model that Web Audio implements is of a series of signal generators, audio file players, and effects processors that can be connected together, much as one might connect a series of modules in an analog synthesizer. The amount of processing that needs to be done is extensive, and from my own experience building synthesizers and connecting them to objects in a game environment with a physics engine, the capacity of the browser to render everything in time quickly degenerates. Recently, an attempt to improve the performance of processor intensive operations has been implemented, and are known as *AudioWorklets*. These are built over a library called *WebAssembly*, where small blocks of code are assembled into machine code, to run at near-native speeds, similar to the speed we expect stand-alone audio applications (DAWs, for example) to operate. Ultimately, this could be a way of bringing native applications and associated speed to the browser. A large program written in C or C++ (such as a DAW) could be run in a browser. It would then be possible to click on a link, and be running sophisticated, fast applications, without having to install them locally. There are cross-platform benefits to this as well, in that maintaining separate code bases for different operating systems would be unnecessary. I will return to what we might extract from this shortly, after a higher layer in the library environment, *Tone js*.

Tone js provides a number of higher-level abstractions familiar to musicians that makes it much easier for a developer to build music applications. Perhaps the most sophisticated aspect of *Tone js* is how it presents musical time, and that is what I will focus on here. Web Audio has an *AudioContext* with an attribute called *currentTime* which, as author Mann points out "starts at 0 when the page is loaded and counts up in seconds." Mann describes a simple musical scenario—starting a sound or song at the push of a button, and in the case of the song, being able to pause, rewind, fast-forward through it as one might in a musical production or listening situation. Pointing out that the continuously increasing nature of the AudioContext currentTime is not particularly useful, or at least clumsy to work with for such a scenario, he includes a transport mechanism to help the coder deal with this:

Tone.Transport provides an abstraction over the AudioContext time which allows you to start, stop and seek within the Transport's timeline. For example you could schedule a bunch of events along this timeline which can be started, stopped, paused, resumed, looped, jump to a specific moment, and even change the global tempo while keeping all those events synchronized. (ToneJs, n.d.)

That idea of being able to change the tempo is a good example of an abstraction being devised to afford the use of musical time concepts by a developer. Javascript code, embedded in web pages, gets run through the Javascript engine within a browser. Each browser implements this in their own way, but meets the language specifications. Browsers are focused on providing users with a smooth visual experience as the main priority. The way that Javascript code runs is not obviously or easily compatible with the most straightforward ways of implementing reliable audio. "Callback" functions that help deal with operations operating in parallel or asynchronously need to be coded to enable anything to occur in time reliably. In the case of *Tone js*, for example, Mann points out how callbacks need to be called slightly in advance of the time at which they are required, so that they maybe scheduled by the more low-level code underneath (the AudioContext time which can schedule audio events to the sample level). This advance period is described as a 'lookAhead.'

At some point, decisions need to be made about the limits of these abstractions. Again, the open-source nature of a library such as this means that users get an opportunity to contribute to the communication around this process. A recent exchange in the email list for *Tone js*, offers a useful example. The library has an object called a *Player* that can play a sample of longer audio file. It can be scheduled in advance, started from a certain point within the file, paused, stopped, reversed, played at different speeds, and so on. The MultiPlayer version of it extends Player so that a single object is able to play a number of different samples on request. A user of the library, a developer, submitted a feature request to the github project issues forum to see if an idea for a particular feature might be considered for implementation (ToneJs 2017). The idea was whether one sample could be "choked" (stopped quickly) if another started. The use case presented was one of a high hat, so that the closed high hat should choke the open high hat and vice versa, matching what would occur with a physical drum kit high hat mechanism. Discussion then ensued as to how and why this might be considered. An owner of a library like this has to decide how to manage their time, and whether to invite a contribution to the code that can be "pulled" in without breaking other parts of the library. People suggesting changes who are capable and willing to write code are obviously preferred over those suggesting changes without contributing, so a kind of hierarchy naturally tends to form in such forums. In this case, a clearly capable developer who had made the decision agreed, along with others, not to implement this at library level, but leave the problem to be solved by developers as needed at the application programming level.

Modern web browsers are complicated environments, and always have been, but for musical purposes their complexity and effectiveness have reached a level that will offer the potential for a great deal more to occur in a browser environment than has been to date. The WebAssembly components are an excellent example of this, with very low level code now being compiled on the fly. That this is occurring in browsers that are used by a huge proportion of computer and phone users is significant.

If the section on time and music languages shows how code infrastructure shapes musical possibilities, then the Web Audio discussion points to musical and commercial probabilities based on resources poured in to engineering particular affordances by some of the world's most influential and powerful organizations in the world today. While motives for broadcasters, freelance developers, startups, and so on might have obvious, direct interests in getting better audio tools, the situation surrounding corporations like Google spending so much time and resources invites further consideration. While standards such as Web Audio may be implemented independently, there is some collaboration. Companies and non-profits like Mozilla (behind Firefox) contribute to and draw on open-source code, although ultimately the code that generates income for Google, Apple, and Microsoft (all browser developers) is closed and proprietary.

A great deal of energy and time is going into effectively duplicating possibilities that already exist in stand-alone software on computers—DAWs, games, utilities. These generally use traditional business models around buying a software as a product although that is changing now with approaches being more subscription based. If more is going on in the browser, then the more data can be collected by companies like Google, for whom that is their means of value as they then target advertising. The rise of audio capabilities in the browser, while convenient for programmers who can relatively easily take very high-level objects and make things without having to have the skills to implement lower level audio operations that programmers used to, can also be seen as another step in the transectorial takeover of music commerce by internet based advertising.

NOTES

1. Singular for our purposes here as there could be several, or many more in a cluster or other large computer.

2. See the *Computer Music Journal* (http://www.computermusicjournal.org/) and *New Interfaces for Musical Expression* (http://www.nime.org/), for example.

Chapter Four

Coding Aesthetics

This chapter explores sound aesthetics in a series of cases where code affordances and constraints as previously discussed are operating. Building from Kirschenbaum, digitally autographic elements provide sonic material that form part of a history of digital sound aesthetics. Glitch and Chiptune provide such examples in this chapter. Although often seen from the perspective of an aesthetics of failure (Cascone 2000) here I want to think about glitch as an aesthetics emerging from the success of error correction software in action. Code has generated new sounds that end up gaining value because they are linked to shared social and musical experiences.

Code also helps connect modern practices with more established sound aesthetics. I explore a situation where code is designed and written to re-create sounds from older sources through guitar amplifier emulation, and software synths. Emulating the sounds of analog and older digital devices reaches back and connects with tools and sounds that have carried considerable cultural capital within the field of music production. I then turn to the closest meeting point of code, coding, music, and associated aesthetics through exploration of live coding. Here, musicians write and modify code on the fly to create live music. The code changes are often projected on to a screen for an audience to be able to see. This is an important conceptual space where the life of code meets life around code. Code and coding is center-stage in this genre. Musical notions of time are connected directly to the way code is created and runs in "realtime." Artists build and modify instruments on the fly as part of creating and modifying the music being made by them that question indexical links between instruments and performers.

Chapter Four

GLITCH

Perhaps the longest standing association between code and sound aesthetics lies in the field of electroacoustic music, that domain of avant-garde practice or art music that uses electronics, including computers, to generate a wide variety of musical works. A good deal has been written about this field (Manning (2004) and Collins and d'Escrivan Rincón (2007), for example), as it has been so critical to changes in musical understanding through experiments pushing aesthetic and conceptual boundaries, many of which have ultimately flowed through to more mainstream musics. Glitch is one such example.

Noise has long been an integral part of sound reproduction technology, from the crackles and pops of wax cylinders and vinyl, to the hiss of tape. Although CD technology was touted as being virtually free from such noise, or at least it was so quiet as to be undetectable, I recall my very first listening experience with the media as unnerving due to noises I did not expect. The music department in which I was an undergraduate purchased early CD players and started collecting disks. I distinctly remember the excitement of listening to orchestral music for the first time on CD, but being unnerved by the occasional, but obvious, clicking and scraping that I could not immediately explain. Later, it occurred to me that the quality of the recording was so high, and the reproduction so noise free, that what I was probably hearing was bow scraping, music stands creaking or moving, and other such noises that one is aware of while in an orchestra, but not when listening from a distance. I have never been distracted by this since, so whether it was just the recording, whether techniques changed to suit the format by placing microphones differently, or it was simply a reaction to a new recording technology I will not know. It certainly did not take long to experience the unique sounds of the format as a result of scratches or marks on the surface of a CD, however. Repetitive clicks, loops, and sounds with a harsh high frequency edge to them became part of the CD experience at some stage or another for almost everyone. These were given the moniker of "glitches" and soon artists were experimenting with these sounds in very deliberate, musical ways.

Glitch has been most commonly explained through a lens of malfunction, as Cascone (2000) expresses in the title of an overview and discussion about the genre: "The aesthetics of failure." Audio glitches are its essential sonic elements and occur as a result of hardware and software failing to render the data read from a CD into an analog audio signal. Engineers, aware of potential inconsistencies in reading data from the disc designed error correction software to avoid playback problems. Engineers today still class glitches as failures, as shown by the Web Audio specification designers:

> Audio glitches are caused by an interruption of the normal continuous audio stream, resulting in loud clicks and pops. It is considered to be a catastrophic failure of a multi-media system and MUST be avoided. It can be caused by problems with the threads responsible for delivering the audio stream to the hardware, such as scheduling latencies caused by threads not having the proper priority and time-constraints. It can also be caused by the audio DSP trying to do more work than is possible in real-time given the CPU's speed. (WebAudio 2021b)

While these software engineers leave no doubt as to their take on the phenomenon, there are other ways of thinking about glitch. Bosma (2016), for example, in examining gender politics points out how masculine the genre has been and how the view from a perspective of an aesthetics of failure reinforces a territorial, conquering and domestication narrative characteristic of many overtly male approaches to art. From this, Bosma reminds us to not focus solely on the text and immediately connected processes, but to constantly situate them in the broader context of human practices, relations and politics: "The discourse of glitch music displays, then, a narrow and abstract vision of digital technology, one that takes into account only the 0s and 1s, instead of the practices and social relations in which these are intrinsically embedded" (Bosma 2016, 107).

One study that does explore this context is that of Prior (2008) in making a case to use ideas from both Bourdieu and Actor Network Theory to better understand such genres towards a more relevant sociology of music.

> The field clearly does set certain limits, particularly in how specific modes of operation and intervention among glitch musicians are played out, but glitch is also held together by an array of other objects which populate these relations and without which the style becomes unthinkable: transistors, electrical pulses, keyboards, software, graphic user interfaces, laptops, CDs, digital signal processing tools, the internet. (316)

There is a long tradition of noise and incidental sounds associated with music technology being used creatively. Bates (2004) describes how glitch fits into a longer span of avant garde and experimental practices, for example, while Sangild (2004) describes the connection of glitch to everyday sonic experience over a particular historical period, and the "fragile sensibility" and unpredictability of technologies that are more usually characterized by descriptions of their efficiency and quality.

Building from this, what if we instead imagine glitch as a result of an aesthetics of success through error correction software working? Or at the very least, what might we gain by proceeding in a vein highlighting the creative use of technology when originally unintended sounds are produced? This alternative perspective can help think through connections between hardware, code, and contexts within which musical aesthetics emerge and transform. Kirschenbaum (2008) and the idea of forensic and formal materiality is useful here. Individual microscopic differences on CDs—their forensic materiality—meant that, despite the early marketing, software running inside CD players was required to recognize and correct errors in playback to give the listener as consistent an aural experience as possible. The code doing this represents an example of formal materiality in Kirschenbaum's model.

For a glitch to sound, whether sporadically or repetitively, at least some of the software is working. Stuart (2003, 48) describes David Ranada, of *Stereo Review* magazine, experimenting with an early CD player by placing increasing amounts of tape on a CD to see what sounds would emerge, and at some point, error correction gave up and the CD tray opened—a kind of final statement and end point for code. Once the CD ejects, the code has stopped. What about all of the error corrections going on that we can't hear? Things are often going wrong at the forensic level when listening to a CD, but we do not hear any artifacts. In this case the error correction code is working as intended. Is that failure? Here we need to think of the criteria around which failure is defined, of course, and the most obvious one in these instances seems to be the transmission of musical sound as originally recorded by the musicians and producers. The point I am really interested in making around failure, is that for us to hear a glitch of some sort, the code is still working in some way. If we think of work like that of Oval where CDs were marked with felt tip pen to create repetitive sonic patterns, the idea of failure becomes even less valuable. Here, Oval is essentially attempting to direct and manipulate error correcting software to respond in particular, patterned ways.

One way of thinking about this, is that new sounds are experienced as unintended consequences of code. Artists in the experimental traditions are often the first to explore such sonic and artistic possibilities. These sounds have occurred for certain generations as parts of once daily listening experiences so the movement of such sounds into more popular contexts is hardly surprising. The unintended consequences of software are similar to the unintended use of amplifiers for distortion, compressors, equalization, and the myriad of practices that help define the aesthetics of technologically mediated musics. Further, that could be code in a context that is not obviously musical. Nonmusical code can have musical consequences.

Allographic consistency is engineered, and artists seek out the unexpected. As those sounds continue as an essential part of musical style, as in glitch, they outlive the technologies that initiated them. Once a sonic aesthetic becomes embedded in aural parts of our lives in important ways, then recreation of those sounds in the most effective manner becomes important.

There are a swathe of glitch plugins available to create these sounds as part of modern music production. Bit crushers are another set of plugins, again re-creating sounds that are part of particular digital histories. So, aesthetics that have become important nostalgically, like those of 8-bit games, or of digital distortion or CD glitches, and that emerged from hardware limitations, are then able to be re-created in software, indeed have to be, as the hardware has improved so far that issues of fidelity have perhaps reached the limits of human perception. The following section on digital emulation explores this in some detail.

DIGITAL EMULATION

As a guitarist, recording musician, and educator of music production, I have long been interested in digital tools that emulate the sound of analog equipment. From guitar amplifiers, effects, studio equipment to vintage synthesizers, numerous emulations are available giving producers, performers, and recordists access to a wide range of sounds for a tiny fraction of the cost of the hardware, and occupying space within a computer, rather than the floor. Software emulation is a thriving space for those building tools for music production. Amplifier emulation software is now widely used in DAWs, for example, and manufacturers of hardware often provide plugins and other software to make their sounds available in different ways.

Wang (2018, 181) in his book on design for music with computers points out that it is tempting to remake what already exists because it is obvious. One of the principles he posits is: "Design things with a computer that would not be possible without," stating "Do not simply copy, port, digitize or emulate. Rather, create something novel and unique to the medium—something that could not exist without it." While this principle makes sense in the more experimental context in which Wang works, the ubiquity, complexity, and span of these emulations indicates a wide range of motives at play for doing exactly what Wang rails against—copying and emulating. This section explores such motives, arguing that emulations demonstrate the encoding of collective aesthetic values, supported by their commercial success, and acting as a form of continuity over an analog-digital transition too often depicted through narratives of disruption.

Although there is much to be gained from a study of emulation focused on interfaces, my aim here is to explore underlying principles, algorithms, and the operation of the code behind them. Unfortunately, most emulations are closed source, making it difficult for a code-centered analysis. In music, however, the connections between academia and industry are tightly enough woven together to draw on open-source examples that can be proven to be closely representative of the operation of closed source versions. The following example of such a connection shows this.

Guitarix is an open-source program for Linux providing guitar amp simulation, and guitar effects. Exploring the source code of this there is a "readme" file clearly linking academic work on emulation techniques and describing in some detail how someone with the appropriate although not inconsiderable skill and knowledge could build one's own amplifier simulation. One thesis titled "Real-time Digital Simulation of Guitar Amplifiers as Audio Effects" in particular stands out (Mačák 2012), in which the author thanks the "Audiffex company for the opportunity to implement algorithms for the simulation of guitar analog effects in their products." Searching for this company on the website kvraudio, a key site for finding music production plugins and other software, reveals a plugin created by them called *multicabinet*, leaving little, if any doubt about the incorporation of the technology described above.

There is a long history of synths, guitar amps, guitar effects, studio equipment, and so on that provide characteristic sonic markers of particular genres, bands, and associated histories. Musicians and music producers develop sometimes strong connections and opinions about the gear they use, for a range of reasons, from their sound, to response, ease and effectiveness of use to name a few. One valued characteristic that appears to be shared by most, if not all, analog music technology is non-linearity. Non-linear refers to situations where a change in output is not proportional to a change in input. The sound of such devices changes in often subtle ways depending on input levels. Guitar amplifier and studio equipment emulation, in particular, attempts to model non-linear characteristics as closely as possible. Schmitz and Embrechts (2013) describe techniques for modeling guitar amplifier cabinets, and included development of a popular plugin format (VST) as part of their work. Pakarinen and Yeh (2009) present an overview of techniques for guitar amplifier modeling focusing on emulating the sound of tubes.

People go to a considerable degree of effort to model that non-linearity as accurately as possible. Doing this comes up against the realtime capabilities of modern computing, considerable though that power and potential is. Analog non-linearity can be extremely complex, so emulation is always an approximation. One of the techniques used is to digitally emulate analog electrical circuitry, then devise mathematical functions that map their input to output relationship as closely as possible. These elements of non-linearity offer sonic modulations ranging from subtle to obvious that contribute to an aesthetics of popular music. Such sounds have been significant in the history of popular music, helping to define particular genres, eras, and associated production techniques.

Among musicians, discussions about cables, tube types, impedances, and so on indicate similar emphases on the value of non-linearity. These musical values are being coded through emulation. Consider the following plugin descriptions from the website of plugin company Acustica Audio:

> Erin represents the state-of-the-art of the plugin suites dedicated to high-end audio mastering. It includes 3 different studio processors embodying the luxury mastering equipment as manufactured by one of the most prestigious designers in the world . . .
>
> Pink is based on a collection of well-known late '60s American studio gear including 6 different EQ models, a super flexible dynamic section, and an iconic console with its 16 line channels and 9 extra custom preamps . . .
>
> Sand reproduces the sonic behavior of a series of high-end British consoles which literally dominated the Pop and Rock scene from the '80s onward. Sound engineers from all over the world swear by their forward, slightly 'aggressive' sound as well as their logical layout. (Acustica, n.d.)

Visual aesthetics are also involved, however, and combine with commercial imperatives to create an appealing product that looks authentic. The plugins are designed to look something like the equipment they are modeled from. The last one called "Sand," for example, is clearly inspired by consoles and channel strips from Solid State Logic—with the "logical layout" a hint, perhaps, if such a thing is needed given the design of the layout, dial style and colors used. Interestingly, SSL who still make consoles, also make plugins.

UAD, makers of a highly valued suite of plugins comes with a fascinating manual, incorporating historical details and descriptions of the multitude of equipment their plugins emulate. The description of their VCA VU, for example, states that "Unlike later monolithic IC units, the "VU" uses a series of discrete components for gain reduction, and therefore has unique nonlinearities not found in other VCA compressors—thus giving it a sonic distinction from later models."

O'Grady (2019) explores the politics of such emulation and draws our attention to the extraordinary detail they go to in order provide as authentic an experience as possible. Perhaps one of the oddest examples of non-linearity modeling is UAD's version of the Harrison EQ where: "Knob settings, when compared to the graphical user interface silk-screen numbers, may not match the actual parameter values. This behavior is identical to the original hardware, which we modeled exactly" (270, UAD Powered Plug-ins, User manual, Software version 5.6).

So, an error on the printing of the parameter values on the original device, is copied exactly. That probably counts more as a quirk, but that is still part of the critical point here. A lot of effort is made to sonically and visually model this vintage equipment. Harrison, who still make very expensive consoles, also make plugins, and have built a DAW based around the open-source Ardour, but with their own proprietary plugins and interface on the mixer section. They describe this as "Fourth-generation Harrison "True Analog Mixing" processing engine with enhanced compressor/limiter algorithms" (Harrison, n.d.).

Emulation goes beyond modeling analog equipment. Hexter, for example, is an emulation of the digital synthesizer the Yamaha DX 7, and the same ideas about modeling quirks are evident. A comment in the source code provides insight into this:

TEXTBOX 4.1: COMMENT FROM LINE 262 IN FILE DX7_VOICE.C (HEXTER, N.D.)

```
/* DX7 envelopes, when rising from levels <= 31 to levels
 * >= 32, include a compensation feature to speed the
 * attack, thereby making it sound more natural. The
 * behavior of some of the boundary cases is bizarre, and
 * this has been exploited by some patch programmers (the
 * "Watergarden" patch found in the original ROM cartridge
 * is one example). We try to emulate it here: */
```

Although these boundary cases from the original were no doubt unplanned, their use by musicians make them valuable, hence the desire to specifically emulate them in this digital version. Another important example of emulations of older digital equipment is with the Fairlight. Such early digital devices created sounds that were heard as new, and certainly had a certain character that was actively pursued by musicians. Indeed, this is something Fairlight co-creator Peter Vogel talks about as to why the Fairlight was popular, and why he thinks it remains so for many to this day (NAMM, n.d.). There is an iPad emulation app to re-create the Fairlight sound today. This forms part of a shifting sound aesthetic and associated discourse linked to music technology.

To go to this trouble appears to have commercial benefits. Not only do established software plugin designers and builders make such software, so do companies building the hardware, from amplifier manufacturers such as Vox to studio equipment companies (UAD). With guitar amplifiers, trademark conflicts are worked around by the use of names that suggest a particular amplifier, while not using the actual brand or model name. Anything with "twin" refers to the Fender Twin, anything with the word "orange" refers to the "Orange" brand of amps (a difficult one to trademark, one assumes), "30" refers to a Vox AC30, and so on.

The central media and associated domains and activities of the "innovating" industry—software in this case—become part of the way the older, more established music industry operates. Code occupies a more central position, even with companies that once exclusively produced and sold hardware. There are various degrees of this, of course. If the opening material one encounters on a website indicates commercial priority, then SSL at the time of writing was very much still a hardware company. Harrison has Mixbus and plugins as the first things one sees, however, followed by digital consoles, and analog at the bottom after some scrolling.

This coming together of hardware and software under the umbrella or organizing goal of a particular aesthetic can be seen as a way of cementing our need for a particular shared aesthetic with acceptance of predominantly software-based workflows for many music producers.[1] Consider Pakarinen and Yeh (2009):

> Although some tube-amplifier enthusiasts might feel that digital emulation is a threat to the tube-amplifier industry, the authors believe that it should rather be viewed as an homage. It can also be seen as a form of conservation, because the quantity and quality of available tube-amplifier components continues to dwindle. After all, the ultimate goal of amplifier emulation is to convincingly reproduce all the fine details and nuances of the vacuum-tube sound, and to make it widely available for use in artistic expression. (98)

In this way of thinking, the folding in of past key sounds and styles is a way of maintaining tradition; not that far removed from particular instrumental and stylistic traditions of music anywhere, but just more focused on technology. The development of emulation demonstrates recognition and an embedding of what is important to particular music traditions developed on stage and in studios over the last fifty or so years. Digital emulation of analog gear therefore provides a connection, a smoother join between analog and digital techniques of music production. Anyone with a Mac and Garageband has access to a range of sounds that draw from the last half-century of recorded music production. Emulations are not sonically perfect in the sense of replication but that is hardly the point; what matters is the tradition of analog sound culture gets pulled into the digital environment and becomes accessible as part of a musical future. For a code musicology, important aspects of the culture around a sound lie in the code that sustains it. There is culture in code.

The digital emulation of the sounds of computer games offers another valuable area for exploration. Sound and music are vital components in computer games, whether played on dedicated consoles, desktop computers, laptops or phones. A key aspect of games is their interactivity, around which new approaches and concepts of musical performance emerge (Miller 2009). Critical work has emerged with art forms built from modified game engines to build theories to guide analysis in the growing field known as ludomusicology (Collins 2013; Kamp, Summers, and Sweeney 2016).[2]

As people spend and have spent significant amounts of time playing games, generational sound aesthetics have ensued. Collins points this out with her recall of the sounds Mario has made from various versions of the Mario Bros games since her first experience of it in 1985. Extensive YouTube activity devoted to old game music and sound reinforces how widespread this is. Hardware constraints have led to software constraints that have determined the kinds of sounds that form part of the historical genealogy of game sounds.

The case of one game, known as "Sopwith" is particularly interesting in this regard. Originally written for the IBM PC in 1984 after the release of its source code some years later, it was ported across to Linux. The sound of the original game used the PC speaker, capable of simple mono sounds by being turned on and off at different rates. Rather than re-writing the sound effects code to use more sophisticated sound card possibilities, the actual behavior of turning a PC speaker on and off is directly emulated in software. The result is that Sopwith sounds very much today like it did in 1984 by simulating dated technology.

Although the Sopwith game example is interesting as an example of sonic nostalgia, the case of Chiptune is more complex, in that new musical genres have been generated (Harlin 2011). Here, music generated from very particular hardware and software constraints, helps generate an aesthetic that forms part of a tradition and has cultural value for a certain group of people. Those sounds then get emulated despite vastly superior sonic possibilities at the time of emulation. The stylistic and technical complexity is described by Reid (2018) where people:

> can compose an expansive range of music, which may adhere to the stylistic conventions of videogame soundtracks of the 1980s and 1990s, or branch into other genre conventions, tropes, and media franchises. We can observe, for example, chiptune (sub)genres of bitpop, 8-bit Reggae and many other mixtures between chipsound and more contemporary—or even other retro—styles; 'authentic' early Nintendo and Game Boy style chiptunes on original microchip hardware; 'fakebit' as larger scale chiptune arrangements utilising modern audio production equipment and virtual emulations of microsound hardware;

and overtly intertextual 8-bit renditions of Phil Collins and 16-bit Super Nintendo imaginings of the theme to the BBC sci-fi television series Doctor Who. (280)

Related is the "Demoscene," stemming from a history of cracked games and software known as "warez," where small groups build demos consisting of audio and visual material using particular constraints extending from an older hardware context. These demos are computer programs with the artistic constraints that they must be written in less than a certain size of code—64 kilobytes or in the more extreme case, less than 4k. The analysis here has centered on the code once written, so code as a text. The following section explores its more active aspect—the process of coding—with an increasingly important musical approach and genre known as "live coding."

LIVE CODING

The most common workflow when coding involves writing, then running. Some languages require a compiler to first take the high-level instructions and compile them into a format to be run, others can be interpreted on-the-fly. In either case, the actions of writing and running are separated. Live coding differs in that it involves on-the-fly writing and editing code that renders music in realtime. A number of specific languages and associated environments exist that are commonly used for this, such as SuperCollider. Live coding is therefore a unique programming *and* musical practice.

One of the features of live coding is that the performance context almost always involves having the code being written and edited projected on to a screen for the audience to see. This is often accompanied with a dynamic visualization of the sound being rendered. The code is on display, as is often the coder via webcam. Live coding opens up dialogues about performance practice, agency, and questions assumptions about the separation of instrument from score.

Live coding performances known as "algoraves" have received media attention as an emerging underground music scene. Amrani and Payne-Frank (2017) in the *Guardian* write about the scene, and produced a short video documentary (Guardian Culture 2017). An observation in the documentary, and one seemingly at odds with coding in general, is that 60–70 percent of the participants and audience were women (see 4:43 in video). As Amrani notes notes, "At the rave, most people—many of them women—were looking up at the projected codes rather than each other. It felt in many ways like an art performance with some dancing, and as my curiosity was satisfied I really started to understand its appeal" (Amrani and Payne-Frank 2017).

In comparing artist/audience communication from the perspective of a more traditional jazz performance background, Cheung (2019, 6) points out that live coding can at times be more like classical music performance with a lack of eye-contact and long periods with little audience interaction. Live coding can involve long periods of an artist typing things on a laptop while the audience listens and looks at the screen projection. Cheung (2019) "noticed that many live coders came from a programming background rather than a professional musician background; many of whom made fantastic, beat-driven, algorithmic and abstract music but perhaps were not coming from a harmonic or melodic approach to their music creation" (2). Nilson (2007, 112–13) describes bouts, duels, and musical 'fights' between live coders on stage, which although presented somewhat light-heartedly, does indicate a particular kind of performance tradition not dissimilar to displays of virtuosity in jazz, hip hop, and other genres where improvisation occurs.

Nilson (2007) describes the process as "the art of programming a computer under concert conditions" (112) which opens up ideas about relationships between traditional forms of musical practice and practicing writing code. Certainly, code writing as practice is foregrounded by live coding. Bergström and Blackwell (2016, 193) explore programming as practice more generally, but specifically look at live coding because of its unique demands connecting code writing with the unfolding of music in time simultaneously. Interestingly, and perhaps slightly out of phase with the more art-music style ideas of performance invoked at times, they state:

> this programming practice is not carried out with the ultimate goal of realizing some design outcome, but is instead a continuous performance, with the journey itself being the principal intended outcome. To stress this point, early live-coding performers often ended their acts by purposefully breaking what they had created: inserting faults into their code, which crash, disrupt or delete their program, ideally producing interesting visual and audio glitch effects as it dies. (193)

Balancing values of musical participation and aesthetic result has been most thoroughly examined from an ethnomusicological perspective. Turino (2009) defines four fields to categorize music making and to help think about how different musical activities are valued—in particular what he describes as "capitalist-cosmopolitan cultural formations." The fields are participatory (where involvement and the act of making music are valued over separate aesthetic value), presentational (a performance for an audience), high fidelity (recordings that index live performance in some way), and studio audio art (electroacoustic music being a prime example). The article focuses on bringing attention to participatory music, a distinguishing feature of which is "that there are no formal artist-audience distinctions, only participants and potential participants" (98). Further, he points out that some forms, such as karaoke, exhibit characteristics of several or all of these fields. While these fields are most useful for comparing styles and values across different societies and cultural groups (97), they can also help us think about historical changes occurring in relationships between repetition, variation, and interaction exposed by live coding:

> These are simply different sorts of artistic activity with different values, functions, constraints, and conceptions of what "music" is and is for. The problem is people typically evaluate the activities and forms of the other fields from the vantage point of the musical field they happen to be invested in—a tendency underwritten by the fact that different societies and cultural cohorts tend to celebrate certain fields over others due to broader habits of thought and value. (109)

The same can be said for evaluating values around the nature of music and how it is constituted, re-constituted, and performed over longer historical periods. These ideas help think through live coding as it is a practice that questions links between repetition, change, instrument, score, performance, and of course writing code that makes music.

The sounds that dominate live coding performances tend to be, as might be expected, electronic, in the sense that oscillators, filters, and effects are combined, as has been the tradition with computer music language composition and electroacoustic musicians since the earliest works in the 1950s and 1960s. Where samples are used, the nature of the languages and their facilities invite particular kinds of experimentation that can easily morph acoustic sounds into more abstract phenomena. Striation is such an example, where fragments of an audio file are extracted, repeated, stretched, and granularized for sonic effect.

Oscar South, in a blog on the main web source for live coding, toplap.org points out how a unique aspect of the form is that performers are creating their instruments on-the-fly. He speaks from the perspective of being a session musician, where one's instrument is well and truly known and skills firmly in place before performance ensues (South 2019). South also describes a workflow that involves preparing scripts in advance to allow a performance to proceed smoothly. This can be compared perhaps to more traditional forms of instrumental practice in jazz and other improvised forms, where the musician can draw from a range of phrases and ideas that have been internalized through rigorous practice. Here, such scripts are both score snippets and instrumental proficiency through practice; both performance and score.

In the second of this blog series South describes the preparation of code to be run later as a script, and then performing with guitars (South 2019b). One of the things about a script like this, is that pieces are not necessarily going to sound the same each time a script is run—it is possible to add choice, randomness, and decision making, all features of algorithmic music more generally. The sequence of things to play collapses into the same media. The instrument looks like the sequence in that they are both in code form, and it is only by reading the code and imagining the results that allow the differences to be abstracted. South also performs with a singer from Siberia, highlighting that this artistry is at the distinctly presentational end of the live coding spectrum (as opposed to the algorave end), with clear artist/audience separation, and complex stage dynamics between performers.

Coding, in styles such as this, can be an important part of musicianship, and form part of a traditional regime and routine similar to instrumental practice. Code is decisive and has agency, although it is an agency ultimately extending from earlier human decisions. Randomness, Markov chains, and other forms of variation are critical elements in live coding, as they are for generative processes increasingly used in electronic music more widely. The rise of code in human music practice also means a rise in a different or extended type of agency, and that means a code musicology needs to examine balances between repetition and variation.

Live coding forces a re-think of this, or at least a re-adjustment of the abstractions involved in the previous examples. Imagine music written, informed, inflected, composed by AI (through code) rendered by more code into audio. Or, what if it stayed in the digital realm and was only "listened" to by MIR to be fed back into the AI? All sorts of fundamental links need to be questioned in such a scenario, and it will be up to a code focused musicology to explore these.

NOTES

1. Not all, by any means, and the rise of hardware in certain domains—synths, for example, speaks to this.
2. See also Oliver (2006).

Chapter Five

A Software Development Perspective

Code is at the center of some of the most ubiquitous tools of music creation. This chapter argues that gaining a better understanding of how this code is created and distributed helps understand how music is often made, and how assumptions, limitations, and workarounds operate. There are disciplinary precedents for this. Studies of music production, perhaps best exemplified by work published by the Art of Record Production organization, have provided important perspectives for popular music studies. Among these, the most relevant from which to shape a code musicology are those that draw out the processes involved in digital production. The idea of "technologically mediated transparency" as posed by Renzo and Collins (2017) is particularly useful here, as is the work on what are described as latent elements in music production (O'Grady 2018). In ethnomusicology, analysis of creative processes in studio spaces and other aspects of production have offered a similar parallel (Meintjes 2003; Bates 2010). This chapter suggests a parallel approach for a code musicology by looking at the significance of software tools in music production and introducing methods to explore their substance.

One of the purposes of the chapter is to offer methodological approaches and areas of analysis many non-developers might not be familiar with. I have chosen two main areas to examine. The first is that of large complicated applications—DAWs—that lie behind so much modern music recording and production. These involve contributions from perhaps hundreds of developers over decades. The second is at the other end of the scale—an app by a sole developer. This explores the idea of appification (Morris and Murray 2018), the highly centralized nature of app distribution, and the close connection between users and developers through the rating and review process.

A critical feature of appification that makes a code musicology widely significant is the way in which such software has spread globally. The highly centralized nature of app distribution, controlled as it is by two giant US-centered corporations, raises questions about diversity, inclusion, and associated discourses of power imbalance. I explore this from the perspective of someone who has tried to develop software in a Global South location often characterized as marginal (Papua New Guinea) aimed at a particular local population (people from the area frequently referred to as Melanesia).

MUSIC PRODUCTION SOFTWARE

In the opening chapters the life cycle of large software projects was mentioned with the observation that many contributing individuals were unlikely to be able to fully comprehend them as systems. DAWs such as ProTools, Cubase, Cakewalk, FL Studio and Logic are all examples of this. They may consist of hundreds of thousands, perhaps millions of lines of C++ code, with some speed critical sections in assembly language, and have been written by many people over a long period; some since the late 1990s. While in the early years of their development only a few people might have been involved, that has changed significantly as they have grown in complexity and have formed cornerstone products of large companies such as Ableton, Avid and Steinberg. This shifting pool of people have worked in teams, in offices, although remote working approaches are increasingly common.

Ableton, the company that develop the DAW and music production environment 'Ableton Live' and associated hardware, offers a glimpse into their working culture in a video titled *Meet the Makers: Ableton Developers at Work* on their website (Ableton, n.d.). We see seminars, discussion, collaboration, and a well-meaning attempt to address obvious gender disparity in the industry. I counted four women at work as software engineers, but a cut to a wider shot of a company seminar shows that they are overwhelmingly outnumbered by thirty or more mainly white men from their mid-twenties on. While the video accents the interesting, varied work life at Ableton, with seminars by luminaries such as Miller Puckette, the opportunity to work on "cool" individual projects, and people from all around the world, the reality is more likely somewhat more mundane and definitely less diverse. Understanding the effects of gendered, cultural, class, and age perspectives on how music software has developed will require the kinds of detailed ethnographies of developer culture such as that undertaken around the open-source movement by Coleman (2013). My purpose here is to propose some methods, approaches that might prove useful in the focused and detailed studies that these crucial matters demand.

One such method is an exploration of what has gone into, and what surrounds, the development of a code base. Romello Goodman, a software developer at the *New York Times,* writes about the context of a code base and how "a codebase is a history of past decisions, assumptions, and compromises" (Goodman 2020). Further, he points out that:

> ... a codebase reflects how teammates communicate with one another. It's a snapshot of our thinking and our best attempts at codifying norms and assumptions. It's a conversation in which each person contributes and is in conversation with those who came before them. With each new feature or bug report, we understand our code better. We identify areas where new logic doesn't quite fit with existing logic. We're constantly in touch with our own past decisions and those of our coworkers. We're working together, trying to harmonize and match one another's thinking patterns and assumptions. We trust one another to make decisions for the good of the team and the organization. Every piece of new code adds to the culture and cultivates our shared understanding. (Goodman 2020)

A code base can appear to be a labyrinthine beast, however, particularly to someone not adept at reading code. It is a snapshot of code at a particular point of time, even if it is a result of historical decisions and coding practices. Goodman reinforces that it is documentation that is key here: "The preservation of decisions and experience is tied to the preservation of our codebase. Even when the code itself is no longer being updated, documentation around the logic or the underlying platform and adjacent technologies can keep a codebase and its culture vibrant."

Fortunately, recording such decisions and documenting the results of discussions and changes to code is almost always, in any serious software project, managed by a version control system. People check code out of a central repository, make changes locally, then submit those changes back to the repository. On large projects that involves those changes being reviewed, accepted (or not), and others can then incorporate those changes into their own local copies. All of this is logged, and can be read by anyone with access to the code. While every single change to the code can be viewed across its entire history, it also contains brief summaries of what has been done.

Closed source applications do not have their git logs on display for anyone other than people in the company with specific privileges and permissions. This protection of IP has obvious commercial imperatives, but we should note the longer term cultural and historical value of these records. Hopefully one day these histories might well form part of an archived history of musical tools, to be made available in a museum of software, perhaps. In the meantime, we must turn to open-source examples that are most likely to offer parallels with and insights into their more commercially secretive relatives. The value of this is reinforced by the fact that people able to build complex software like open-source DAWS often have commercial experience and themselves point out how similar the working processes are.

ARDOUR

In the world of DAWs, the closest open-source example we have is Ardour. It has been in existence since 2000, is written mainly in C++, has had a number of developers, although has been and still is centered around the key figure of Paul Davis. Ardour is a fully featured, stable, open-source DAW that was first released in 2005. This is a large code base involving numerous programmers, many of them professionals.

Davis was interviewed in 2015 by the author of a long running music tech blog, Darwin Grosse, an employee at music software company Cycling74 (Grosse 2018). Davis worked as a programmer in research and commercial environments, and was the second employee at Amazon. He left after a year, and has coded audio and music ever since. In discussing the origins of Ardour, Davis describes how he had bought an audio interface (an RME Digiface) in 1999, but as a Linux user, had to write a driver to be able to use it. He also realized there was no actual recording software under Linux, so set out to code Ardour.

Written as a digital tape machine, he had something running in a month or two. Editing abilities were then needed, and he realized the immensity of the task before him. As an open-source project that has been running ever since, he estimates between 50 and 60 programmers have been involved across a very wide spectrum of abilities. Robin Gareus, a developer who has made significant contributions to Ardour, and whose PhD thesis (Gareus 2017) deals with the complexity of latency compensation in the application states that the program has over 650 000 lines of code, and that it is not unexpected to have more than 5000 bugs in such a code base (154).[1] One key developer, David Robillard, was working at Ableton at the time of the interview. Robillard has a PhD in computer science and writes open-source music software in addition to commercial software, reinforcing the point made earlier about close connections between software engineers in the proprietary and open source domains.

Harrison, a company known for its mixing consoles, has combined its own proprietary code with Ardour for sale as a DAW. Known as Mixbus, Harrison includes its own signature EQ, various effects such as compression and tape saturation, as well as a built-in bus configuration modeled on their analog devices. One of the huge benefits of open-source software is that, as the name suggests, it is simple to get a copy of the source and read it, giving us a taste of what many large proprietary projects might look like.

One of the most commonly used version control systems is known as *git* and was written to better manage a particularly complex development process—that of the Linux operating system. Ardour uses git, and every time someone makes a change to the code, there is a log of that change, along with when it was made, who did it, what was changed, and a description by the developer responsible. Git logs are a critical text pointing to the code base, how it was made, who was involved, and allows a reader to explore changes that were made at any single point in the development process (or "commit" as the smallest unit of recorded change is known as). Git has sophisticated built-in capabilities for searching and summarizing.

My intention was to read through the git log of Ardour, and see if I could get a sense of how software like this takes shape, and how the people behind it interact. I soon found myself bound up in the detail of individual "commits" and it was difficult to get a sense of broader structural decisions and shape. Searching for keywords was valuable in seeing how many times and in what context "ProTools" was mentioned, or exploring the interaction with Harrison, for example. Git commands allow summarizing of the data such as who has been involved and how many commits and lines of code per developer. The command "git shortlog-sn" summarizes the people that have made commits, and orders them by the number made. That revealed about 160 names, of which less than 10 appeared to be duplicates. The majority had one or only very small numbers of commits. I recognized hardly any women's names, although there are obvious difficulties trying to establish this given some people use nicknames. It is also possible to delve into the number of lines created and removed by individual contributors. Paul Davis, for example, as of writing had added 3.8 million lines of code, and deleted 1.75 million. A quick examination of the top twenty or so contributors indicates the core group of developers, and the extraordinary amount of work over a long period of time that goes into creating and maintaining such code.

While the exercise was not particularly enlightening for me in getting a sense of how Ardour has been designed, and how changes have been decided on, it has shown social, communicative aspects around the development process, including dialogue, humor, and sarcasm mixed in with the quotidian, straightforward statements of changes made. Design discussions appear as though they must be taking place elsewhere—a developer mailing list, and specific IRC channels in the case of Ardour—and these would be useful sources of analysis.

At the other end of the music software complexity spectrum lie apps, sometimes written by a single developer within a short period of time, and it is to my own example of that as a developer I now turn to.

TWOTRACK

I recall becoming captivated by my first Android smartphone in 2010, as I explored the range of things it could do beyond being a phone. In particular, I tried various music utilities such as tuners, metronomes, and recorders, but soon felt the need for a simple multi-track recorder that would allow me to play my guitar, record it, then record over this as an overdub. Existing apps seemed too complicated, as though they were duplicating more sophisticated desktop software. I felt there was a gap for something simple, and set about learning to write apps for the Android platform. I came up with the idea of Twotrack—just a simple record, then "bounce" process, a technique common in the days of tape, where multiple tracks were mixed together to one track, therefore freeing up a track or tracks for more overdubbing. The recording apps I had tried used compressed audio formats, and I was interested in trying uncompressed formats (such as wav files used in DAWs) so that multiple bounces would not end up in reducing the quality of the mixed tracks. The idea was also that this would allow easy importing of recordings made on the phone to computer DAW software. I aimed for a simple workflow and interface, hoping that non-recording musicians would be able to easily take up the idea, thus giving me a bigger potential market.

I spent several months coding this in my spare time, and released Twotrack to the Google Play app store in July 2012. I eagerly waited for others to try the app, and despite my first review "It sux—don't buy it" (it was free!) within a few weeks hundreds of people had tried it out, and some became frequent users. Fast forward to the time of writing, and nearly half a million people have tried it, with hundreds of people using it every day in 198 countries. In fact, according to the stats collected, the only countries in which it has not been used are Djibouti, Equatorial Guinea, Guinea-Bissau, Comoros, Eswatini, and Vanuatu. The app is free, and I earn small amounts of money from it through Google's AdMob network which is owned and run by Google. As of March 2019 it had delivered about 11.5 million ad impressions. Clicks on 0.4% of those have earned me daily amounts anywhere from a few cents to a cup of coffee, and very occasionally a cheap lunch.

I have never trained formally as a software engineer but have been programming since the mid-1980s mostly as a hobby. That changed rapidly in 1999 while working at the University of Papua New Guinea. My growing interest in Linux had been recognized by senior colleagues, and due to a funding and staffing crisis I was called in to manage a troubled university IT department rapidly trying to move a student database from an old mainframe system to allay fears of damage from any Y2K bugs as the new millennium ticked over. Outside contractors that had been assigned the task did such a woeful job that I had to rapidly patch together scripts written in the programming language Perl to access a modern database using data from the mainframe, with a web interface. The experience of having to ship a working software product under pressure has subsequently been very useful, and I have drawn on this in designing and writing software for users to annotate audio and video content, and of course Twotrack among other projects.

In all of these projects, it is often the navigation of quirks, workarounds, library compatibilities, and of course bugs that occupies a considerable amount of programming time. For Twotrack this includes managing an app's life cycle within the operating system, and inadequacies with the audio performance. In the process of building the app, I quickly came across the unreliability and extremely poor performance of Android when it comes to audio latency. Had the latency just been long, I could have easily adjusted the recording position after each recording, but what was most difficult to deal with was the inconsistency of the latency. This is due to underlying infrastructure of the Android code base, so that other applications suffer performance hits while other background apps and tasks for the operating system work. Although I coded a latency adjustment setting, and documented how to use this, the inconsistency meant that I also needed to implement the ability for the user to nudge an overdubbed recording back and forth by varying amounts to line up recordings appropriately.

App Distribution Systems

One of the most significant features of the appification of smartphone software is the approach to centralized distribution through the tools and sites that connect developers to users—the app stores. These are the places where apps have been categorized and ranked by algorithms, where people search, install, and have the opportunity to offer ratings and provide feedback. Developers have their own interface and portal that connects their work to the app store. This system provides another view of ratings, bug tracking, an ability to provide updates, a means to respond to user comments, track how many users there are and how they interact with an app through "analytics," and enable the provision of text, graphic and video assets that form the content on the app store that users see. It is also where the app store owners decide what is acceptable, set agreements, monitor, connect the developer with an actual person or company, and implement payments. These are the key sites for exposing the nature of communication around this type of software.

For smartphone apps to make it to the biggest audiences most easily, code is compiled and submitted through the developer console for consideration to be released. The developer adds a description, information about the audience and appropriate content, and, if all goes well, the app appears over a period of hours to a potential audience of billions in hundreds of countries. There are millions of apps, so a new one tends to be obscured until it can be marketed or rises in prominence in various other ways such the app store algorithm. When people search for apps, an algorithm ranks apps under various categories. This includes rating, number of downloads, how often it is updated, and so on. User and developer activity including the number of ratings, and whether a developer responds to individual comments all appear to play a part in that ranking. This represents an unprecedented connection made available to anyone able to write appropriate code and go through the relatively straightforward set of steps to release it.

People then download, try out the app, and sometimes comment and leave a rating. A developer can then read this and from within the developer console, respond. Extensive information can be gathered by developers from online users. Some of this is available in realtime. Although anonymized for the developer, one can still see the location (at city level at least), device type, demographic info, interest areas, usage patterns, and length of engagement. A developer can choose to measure how often a particular user interface element is selected or pressed, as well. While ostensibly that information is presented to assist the developer in making better apps, providing better experiences, and responding appropriately and rapidly to any problems, it also provides a fascinating insight into the astonishing data that Google, in this case, is amassing. For music, as more mundane acts such as sharing and listening are carried out on phones, the repository of information about what people are doing is potentially very detailed.

Smartphone apps can prompt the user to send a message to the developer, along with any relevant log information if an application crashes. Developers can access this and respond accordingly. Data is also gathered as to the kind of crash and how often. Crash data can also be collected as part of the analytics system. So this represents a form of direct communication between users and developer, and allows for potentially rapid (as in days, even hours) cycles of response.

The Economics of Twotrack

App development can be a very time intensive task, and for me as something done on weekends and evenings in any spare time, I was keen to explore remuneration possibilities. The dynamics and competition means that free apps are the standard, and for Android at least, is what people expect, and certainly for an amateur developer like me, unable to fix bugs particularly regularly, it was clear that a free app with ads was the best compromise. I experimented for a while with a paid version of the app, charging a couple of dollars for a version with no advertisements, but being unable to adequately provide support, I felt this was not a responsible approach.

Because there are so many apps in the respective marketplaces it is important that developers pay attention to the quality of their listing on the store to ensure the algorithm that ranks apps works in their favor. A number of businesses have emerged to ostensibly assist developers. Search Engine Optimization (SEO) is an important part of this, with companies such as App Annie offering free and paid services to provide data and suggestions for keywords and phrases that might improve search rankings in the app stores. The actual details of how these algorithms work is unknown outside of Google, but according to companies offering services to optimize for search, it involves numbers of downloads, the number of installs versus uninstalls, retention, ratings, reviews, and stability and performance. These SEO companies rely on developers subscribing to their premium services for ranking information, and search engine optimization tips. I have also been offered services, usually through invitations by individuals, to buy 5 star reviews, as the rating can affect the ranking. Google also offers paid services to developers, such as its translation service to get developers to localize into as many languages as possible.

An important component of the developer console is the access it provides to anonymized data about where, how, and how often the app is being used. One of my favorite views of such data is a map of the world, with spots lighting up as data collected in the last few minutes is presented. The console also provides crash reports, describing the version of Android, the model, number of users impacted, and so on. A "stack trace" is also provided, which is a kind of list of what happened and the machine state as the bug caused the application to crash. Data is presented as to where one's app sits in relation to peers; other music and recording apps in this case.

In the app environment, a direct connection linking users with developers is created through the ratings and comments section. There are public facing reviews and ratings, along with developer responses. Users who have made a review have an opportunity to respond, edit their comments, and adjust their rating. The console allows developers to monitor incoming reviews, respond

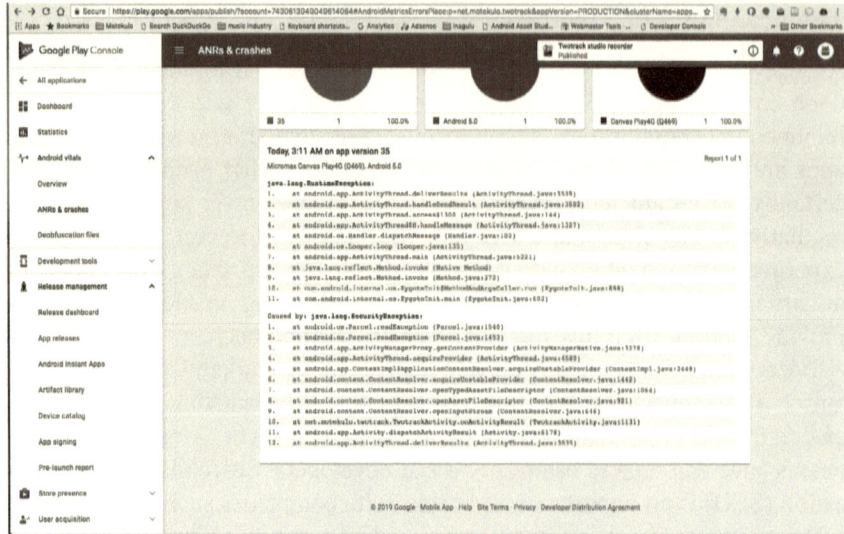

Figure 5.1. Crash report from Google Play Console; screenshot of the author's Google Console account

to them, and track changes in the average score. The reviewing process has also led me to email exchanges where it has become clearer what users are doing with the app.

The rating forms part of the algorithm for ranking the app within the store, so acting as an incentive for developers to try and improve apps and attend to user concerns and feedback. The app store rating and review process is quick, and less formal. That said, for Twotrack at least, only about 0.6 percent of users rate the app, and fewer still at 0.2 percent write anything. As of April 16, 2019, the app had a rating of 3.485, having had 2357 ratings, of which 979 had left comments (reviews). Anybody who leaves a review has taken time to do so. An effort is involved. As a developer, I feel some gratitude to anyone who has taken that time, no matter how low the rating or unpleasant the review. Some reviews seem likely to be people venting their frustration, as they simply make derogatory comments without any real reasons given. I have an email address that users can contact me through, and this has led to some useful, cordial, ongoing exchanges. Some of these emerged from difficulties and frustrations the user was having, and many seemed grateful that someone had replied at all.

Feedback in the first year or so ranged from statements of obvious frustration and perhaps anger—"Fuck this app BS"[2]—to " Good Its excelent I've bin searching for something like this for a while no if you are a music lover install it."[3] Frustration and anger are clearly evident with comments like "Tracks get destroyed! You need to fix this app badly it will make amazing recordings then out of the blue distort the song terribly i wanna crush my phone i get so pissed!!! Ill give u a million stars if ya could fix that."[4] A user, obviously frustrated, but also recognizing and targeting the developer (me) with "This app sucks ass who ever made dis is shity fuck dis bitch ass app ade dis is shity fuck dis bitch ass app."[5]

Reviews are often left that aim to assist other users in deciding whether or not to bother downloading, such as "Abysmal This app is shit to say it nicely. Im gonna try to find one that actually works. GO BACK TO THE DRAWING BOARD ON THIS ONE BOYS."[6] The assumption that there are a number of males working as developers is congruent with wider assumptions stemming from the reality of the app development world. Most apps are developed by teams of men. People sometimes refer directly in the review regarding experiences with the developer, so that the term 'dev' seems widely understood colloquially. In replying to users, I have often been tempted to use the term 'we' when replying, as though I am part of some bigger app development studio, rather than a single independent hobbyist.

Many of the most useful reviews are those with ratings in the middle of the range such as "Good start, needs work. On my Samsung gt p6810 running old android, this app has a fail when the screen rotates. A copy and paste function would be cool, or a loop—so i can freestyle over a short section of beat for ages. Good work tho, i mean, considering its free :-)."[7] Here, the device model, an attempt at the version of Android, specific bugs, and a compliment are all wrapped together.

The longest review so far is 340 words long; coherent, polite but frank, and a list of suggestions to improve stability and the user experience.[8] This was received at a time when I was busy on fieldwork in Papua New Guinea with a poor internet connection and the demands of work and life meant I did not reply within a reasonable period of time. To get an idea of the sort of detail considered by this particular reviewer, a suggestion was made to fix the "mix" function, a key concept in the app where the overdubbed track is mixed down with the master track, leaving the overdub track free for further recording. Accidentally hitting the mix button has caused problems for a number of people:

> When I'm skipping forward on an overdub track, it's way to easy to accidentally hit mix. And there are two times now where I'm sure I never hit the button but it mixed anyway. Three different times, the app suddenly stopped and android asked me to close it or wait, I waited but it was frozen, so I closed it and when reopened it, it mixed my overdub. All of these occurrences caused me to lose all my work ugh! So please fix mixing issues. Here are some ways to prevent accidental mixing. 1.) Move mix button so it's under the "more settings" button,

the one that looks like."..." 2.) Add pop up confirmation 3.) Get rid of button and make user grab the whole overdub track with finger and slide down to main track to mix . . . this would be very difficult to do accidentally. 3.A) make the button different so it's harder to do on accident, like a slider button, or a combination of buttons, like I slide a button to enable mixing, then I press the mix button.

Another detailed review, at 3 stars, states: "This could be such a great app. So much potential. It is exactly what I needed: just a pocket recorder with multitrack functionality without bloaty features I don't need taking up RAM—well, kinda. It's pretty buggy. So let's make some constructive criticism and say what would make this a 5 stars app." There is then a useful list of five detailed UI suggestions, including a request for an ad-free version. It ends with "Regardless of everything, thanks for making this free app for the world. :)."[9]

There are a number of concerns about timing errors due to latency inconsistency (and length) (Appendix 2, items 16, 3, 17, 18). Indications that people are rapping over imported mp3 tracks (id16), recording acoustic guitars multiple times and voice (Appendix 2, item 18). The open-source desktop application Audacity gets mentioned a couple of times in the reviews, with people exporting the wav file, then working further in Audacity on a laptop or desktop computer. Someone else stated that they import recordings into their mixing software on a desktop (Appendix 2, item 19). Some comments express gratitude only, recognize developer response (21), and have clear ideas about what is reasonable for apps in terms of data collection: "No weird permissions or persistent background processes, this is how android should be" (20).

There are bug reports (22) and low ratings for when things do not work (23). Part of the problem with Android here is the difficulty in testing, as there are thousands of devices; it is simply not possible to test on them all, just on as representative a subset of OS versions and screen sizes as possible. Some people have provided tips aimed at other users such as turning off the auto-rotate screen and disabling sleep modes (1). At the more paranoid end of the scale, one reviewer suggested that, after the app froze, that perhaps it was malware/spyware and another expressed concern over data collection with "Im not sure Sometimes it sends the wrong recording through bluetooth idk is some one listening to the recordings" (id2).

As the app has moved well beyond English speaking populations, reviews in a variety of languages have been received, along with an automatic translation provided by Google. These have been in German, French, Spanish, Portuguese, Russian, and Thai. In my experience, it is particular kinds of users from particular places with common language skills to me that are easiest to respond to. This will be explored further in the chapter exploring smartphones. Autotranslate from a language I don't speak can make it very difficult, even impossible to respond to in the same way. There is already a built-in favorable bias for the comments and ideas of people speaking the same language as the developer.

The developer console for Google Play allows developers to setup A/B tests of the app store presence on the site, and to then compare statistics and decide how to best present apps in terms of graphics, descriptions, keywords, and so on. There are hundreds of different phones and tablets that run Android, compared to the Apple only stable for iOS. That means a great deal more variation in hardware specifications and capabilities, although basic standards need to be met.

My own development process and organization of time tends to revolve around work and other commitments. As a result, long periods have often occurred where I have not updated the app, and where changes in the operating system code have meant that various functions have stopped working, or cause crashes. Through March and April of 2019, the performance of Twotrack had fallen to an extent that I decided action was needed, so through a number of updates I attempted to improve the performance through bug fixing and adjusting code to accommodate new API changes in the operating system.

BUILDING FOR THE NEXT BILLION

While the majority of my users are in the US and other Global North locations, the fact that people in almost every country in the world have used my app is a personal insight into the way that smartphones represent the spread of computing globally, and in this case, musical computing. Google recognizes this better than anyone with the kind of data they collect, and on a page aimed at app developers titled "Build for the next billion users" there is the following statement:

> The pace of smartphone growth around the world is unprecedented, helping billions of new users come online for the first time. However, a majority of users in these markets face constraints not commonly seen in developed markets, such as: limited access to data connections and high costs when they are available, devices with reduced memory and smaller screen sizes, and prepaid accounts topped up as means permit. To address the needs of these users, apps need to be aligned closely with local commerce, culture, and language—more so than might be necessary when targeting developed markets. (Android, n.d.)

Google reminds app developers in building for the next billion that they will be "diverse in every respect: their location, cultural experience, computer expertise, connectivity access, and the kinds of devices they use" (Google, n.d.). Developers are urged to develop for low bandwidth, low end phones, use less data, allow offline usage and so on. My own development experiences speak to these matters as the following example demonstrates.

I have been observing and writing about the production of music, and the technology involved, in Papua New Guinea and other nations collectively known as Melanesia since the mid-1990s. The advent of cell phones, and later smartphones and their effects on music distribution and listening practices have been significant (Crowdy 2015; Crowdy and Horst forthcoming). This work has tended to focus on what people have been doing with phones, and ideas about limited data connections and use of older phones resonated. It wasn't until developing an app and testing and trying to build it in Papua New Guinea that I encountered what I see as a fundamental flaw in Google's perspective that speaks to bigger issues of power imbalances between the Global North and South.

As an output from a group research project exploring social and economic justice related to uses of cell phones for music in Melanesia, I worked with an NGO to support their objective to educate and communicate widely around non-violent means towards West Papuan self-determination.[10] Widely ignored by international organizations, perhaps because of fears of offending powerful Indonesian interests and American gold mining investments, indigenous West Papuans have been calling and fighting for autonomy for decades. Working with NGOs and musicians closely aligned with communicating news of their plight, our grant decided to create and release an app that would communicate testimonies and other information and music about a massacre on West Papuans by the Indonesian military in July 1998. On the island of Biak in 1998 Indonesian military forces opened fire on peaceful protesters, killing many. A booklet was written by the NGO we worked with, documenting testimonies from survivors, and we also produced, with partner organization Wantok Musik, an album of spoken word and musical testimonies performed by survivors of the massacre, other West Papuans ni-Vanuatu and indigenous Australian musicians.

I packaged this material together in an app titled Byak and released it to the Google Playstore. The app was developed using what is known as a hybrid html5 framework, which allows it to be relatively easily built for various platforms, mainly the web, Android and iOS. I focused on Android, as that is what the vast majority of people in Melanesia use. I traveled to Papua New Guinea with research colleague and digital anthropologist Professor Heather Horst for a third field trip around this project in September 2019. We took a draft version of the Byak app with us, with the aim of carrying out some testing, getting feedback, making modifications, and so on. We tested the app by giving it to various Papua New Guinean research participants in both the capital, Port Moresby, and a village some 100km or so to the southeast.

Although internet access is widespread in Port Moresby, it is very expensive. There was also data coverage in the village we visited, although it was so slow that to download more than a few pictures was difficult, full of interruptions, and impractical. People use apps such as ShareIt, which create local wifi hotspots allowing phones to share files, including apps. We used this to share our Byak app, as downloading a 20–30mb app from the Google Playstore was expensive in Port Moresby, and extremely impractical (but not impossible) in the village.

As soon as the first few tests were over, it became very clear that some simple changes would need to be made. I planned to make these in the evening in my hotel room when in Port Moresby, then upload a new version of the app to the Google Play Store. The Android Studio application is an integrated development environment (IDE) that takes care of updating libraries, and keeping all of the various dependencies required by the app to build and run. It became immediately apparent, in my expensive hotel room in Port Moresby, that because of the internet and network infrastructure it was simply impossible to download the updates to build the app, and equally difficult to upload a large file.

There is a way of setting the application up to operate in an offline mode, but it requires downloads in the first place before that is possible. I was essentially stuck with no way of updating the app via the means provided by Google. In the end I was able to find an offline alternative by bypassing the IDE and using the command line. I could then transfer a compiled application to a phone using the ShareIt application. It seemed to me that the engineers developing these tools had never actually experienced the internet as many in the Global South do. On a previous trip the year before, I had met a Papua New Guinean software developer who had written a streaming app for Christian music, and he had pointed out how navigating these matters was a fundamental part of software development in such an environment. He was working at the time for one of the main telecommunication companies in PNG, one known for the fastest internet speeds in the country, so was himself in a situation of some relative privilege. It wasn't until I had experienced this myself, however, a year or so later, that the true impact of his words hit home.

Reflecting on Google's statement that opened this section, it is clear that the focus is on "us" as Global North fast internet developers developing for "them," a potential huge customer base, over there in the Global South. What is perhaps needed is developing as, and with, the next billion. While Google's exhortations to consider the next billion may well be realistic for developers in the Global North, or more connected parts of the Global South, there is a good deal more to be done to enable effective development for the next few thousand developers. While there might well be pockets of people in Google and other corporations with genuine interests in improving the possibilities for developers in the Global South, ultimately, and hardly surprisingly for an advertising company, the spiel is really about ways to engage with a billion new customers from the comfort and privilege of a Global North development environment.

Sectorial Transformation

By placing the creation and maintenance of code at the center of examination, two important areas emerge that a code musicology must engage with when asking what does all this mean for music? With software at the center of music production, distribution, and use a code musicology must ask questions about the concentration of power (male, Global North) in the creation of music software. Are there musical hierarchies being built as that concentration of power renders our tools for making music? Are certain musical concepts and approaches to rhythm, harmony, structure prioritized over others? What might the musical consequences be around diversity, kinds of activities, access?

In a wide-ranging collection exploring what they call 'appification,' Morris and Murray (2018) point out how App stores have been notable for "crystallizing a certain definition of apps that has come to shape how we think of the relationship between software and ourselves" (4). They point out how while apps are part of a longer history of software, they present configurations and connections across a wide spectrum of user inputs, activities, and locations; far more than boxed software from computers, certainly. Further, they are designed largely around the aggregation of micro-data from simple activities. Apps are written to carry out single or simple tasks and this is part of their distinctiveness as a category of software (Morris and Elkins 2015).

Twotrack is an example of this in attempting to distill essential aspects of multi-track recording to something simpler to be used by many. The more people able to use the app, the more advertising can be broadcast, and more data collected. There are a number of other aspects to the model of commerce that are design related worth thinking about here.

Part of the startup based entrepreneurial milieu within which apps have emerged has been the idea of releasing a product in app form as quickly as possible, leading to the idea of a 'minimum viable product' (MVP). This is then refined and changed through incremental updates. Razlogiva (2018) points out how the music recognition app Shazam moved from being open source to closed and proprietary, fulfilling a different purpose to channel users to buy music. Brunton (2018) shows how through incremental updates, again often based on commercial imperatives, apps such as WeChat change and wield influence that serves as forms of societal infrastructure (182). While apps are often free, or low cost, they are commodity forms built to advertise, selling more features ('freemium') or collect data. As Shepherd and Cwynar (2018) suggest ". . . what is mundane about apps may not so much be the software but, rather, the manner in which the devices themselves have become so deeply ingrained in everyday life as a portal for commercialization spurred on by venture capital" (177).

The case of Yik Yak, a discontinued social media app based on threads within a radius of one's physical location, demonstrates how the funding and commercial model is part of the whole process; startups create something novel and need to grow rapidly; novelty and funding reinforce:

> The app industry's funding model facilitates this by making an abundant amount of capital available early on during the novelty phase. In this cycle, the novelty and the funding reinforce each other until the novelty wears off, growth stalls, and the funding dries up. This, in turn, necessitates the adoption of increasingly drastic design measures that often serve only to hasten the app's demise. (177)

In this environment, and along similar lines, musical activities are as likely moulded and driven by commercial imperatives characteristic of the format and dominant commercial models of apps as they are by a desire to deliver effective musical functions.

Centralization

The diversity within app stores is in inverse proportion to the diversity of app stores themselves. The app stores present a scenario that offers the lure of entrepreneurial individual success, but ultimately access is controlled by Apple and Google. The potential to release an app independently from use of the Play Store exists, but the visibility of the app is greatly reduced as a result. There is no effective way for most developers to bypass either Google or Apple as gatekeepers. Only large, hugely popular apps like Fortnite by Epic Games can realistically distribute content outside of those stores.

Even Epic Games come across difficulties, however, while arguing that it was too difficult for users to go through their own download process that bypassed Google's Play Store (Smajstria 2020). Facebook also experienced a similar wielding of power when a change in Apple policy stopped the operation of a number of internal iOS apps the company used (Warren and

Kastrenakes 2019). This kind of power emerges in the media because of the relative size of the corporations involved and ways in which their histories have clashed, interlocked, and competed. For smaller players such as independent developers, however, such struggles are not nearly so widely communicated.

Google and Apple end up controlling access to their distribution channels quite tightly and set particular parameters as to the sort of apps that can be published. There are a number of elements to this. What is essentially immediate access to a global audience of billions comes with compromises. Google sets a range of criteria that developers need to adhere to. I discovered this while making an update to our Byak app for iOS. Although the app had been reviewed and accepted initially, on attempting to update the app, it was rejected, with a statement about the content being more book-like (despite a significant part of the app being musical recordings—an album in effect) and a suggestion we remodel the content with Apple's iBook software and submit it as a book, not an app.

Apps rely on a familiar model with massive amounts of varied, diverse, user content all concentrated into the hands of a few companies. The app store model for Google and Apple is not that different to YouTube and other sites where users provide the content. In this case, developers provide content to Google to skim 30% and provide a massive potential audience but one needs to navigate a visibility problem among numerous other apps in the same category to have any chance of succeeding. Even if lots of people do end up using those apps, the income is minimal. Apple and Google are really selling a dream that only a small subset of developers really benefit from in any meaningful way in terms of income.

The rhetoric surrounding development of apps is one of individual or small group creativity and labor with the possibilities as effectively limitless. Interviews with developers feature on both "meet the developer" posts within app stores (Apple, for example) and in material created by Google aimed at developers, online and at conferences and events aimed at developers. The reality is developers are content providers, just like YouTube video uploaders. The controversy surrounding ridiculously low royalties to musicians from services like Spotify suggest that a similar model is at work there as well.

Another aspect of the oligopoly control over the apps used by billions of people is the data generated. To some extent the public is still in the nascent stages of imagining what that data might be used for, but the collection of so much data by such a small number of players demands attention. For our purposes here, what sort of data collection might matter when music is being considered? As a developer, the information I get from Twotrack is anonymized. I might see on the "streamview" location (to city/town resolution), device, time used, and so on, but Google necessarily collects identifying data. The significance and implications of that are far-reaching, and the next chapter explores that. For perhaps the first time in human history, it is possible that detailed information, identifiable to the individual, from the digital creation of music (assuming made on a phone) followed by its distribution, associated discussion, modification, and so on could be held by a few corporations.

NOTES

1. For information on numbers of lines of code in various projects see https://www.visualcapitalist.com/millions-lines-of-code/ and https://www.informationisbeautiful.net/visualizations/million-lines-of-code/.
2. Rating of 1 from 2013-06-02T21:51:16Z.
3. Rating of 5 from 2013-08-03T19:16:40Z.
4. Rating of 1 from 2013-09-01T22:53:18Z.
5. Rating of 1 from 2013-09-17T16:01:17Z.
6. Rating of 1 from 2014-01-19T00:35:17Z.
7. Rating of 4 from 2013-08-14T10:38:08Z.
8. Received 2017-06-07T15:32:54Z.
9. Received 2018-09-02T22:57:26Z.
10. Australian Research Council Linkage Grant, LP150100973, "Music, mobile phones and community justice in Melanesia."

Chapter Six

Code on the Move

This book started with an example of listening using a phone and Bluetooth headphones to highlight data movement. This chapter examines that in more detail and looks at the significance of the key devices responsible for the global spread of this phenomenon—smartphones. Placing code at the center of this discussion foregrounds smartphones as globally distributed *codejects*. Only when the code they contain runs, in fact, are they smartphones at all. Putting code at the center of a data discussion is slightly more complex, in that one of the main metaphors widely used—that things get moved—obscures more elaborate and abstract operations. A brief discussion of those actions is therefore useful.

For data to appear to be moved across a network, it is first broken into smaller packets. Each of those is then assigned information as to its order in relation to its fellow packets, and an address to where it is going. It is then copied across to a router, whose job it is to check a list of known addresses, and if known forward it on, or if not, to pass the packet higher up the router chain until the address is known. Note that nothing is really moved as a physical thing might be; a representation of it as a signal is copied elsewhere. At the destination address, packets are received and re-combined into the original chunk of data. If any packets have failed to arrive a request is made for them to be re-sent. A coherent copy of the original then appears at the destination. Like the earlier discussion of a music file, processes of fragmentation and re-ordering are at the center of how this works. Once again, music as a phenomenon that is ordered in time gets cut up, transferred, and put back together again as a matter of routine.[1]

Splitting, fragmenting, sending, deciding, forwarding, receiving, re-combining, correcting, requesting, and re-sending; all of these are actions carried out by code. Little wonder then that we conveniently refer to this complex of activities as movement of information. There is a lot going on that we ordinarily do not need to know about. This is important conceptually for a code musicology in connecting these same processes of fragmentation, duplication and re-combination that occur around musical activity at higher levels. Drawing on wider phenomena where the collection and use of data is central, Koutsomichalis (2016) explore the idea that we are in an age of "Big Music":

> to listen in the age of big music is to traverse an inexhaustible data-space, employing a series of interfaces, and being driven by intelligent recommendation systems and social networking. Even the simplest listening act requires at least a service provider (e.g., YouTube, SoundCloud), a network client (e.g. a web browser, Facebook), a hardware terminal (e.g., a laptop, smartphone, smart TV) and an audio reproduction system (e.g., headphones, loudspeakers). Each of these layers imposes particular schemata according to which content may be navigated, performed and phenomenologically embodied. (25)

A simple act of sharing music in the form of a recording involves a complex trans-industrial network, computer hardware and software in the form of a smartphone, a relationship with a phone company, money, and an account with a relevant platform. Your data travels and is held by a third party, possibly in another country. Data is collected about your activity, as that is where the value lies in this activity for the corporation involved. I want to reinforce why the movement of data in particular ways associated with modern platform based capitalism marks a key conceptual pivot.

First consider local file sharing, not involving the internet, something common before the emergence and growth of streaming services, where people owned music files, whether purchased or collected in other ways. This requires co-location of the sharers, and via the Bluetooth protocol data travels wirelessly, locally, and reasonably securely between two paired devices. With data on portable media, people need to be co-located as well, to actually physically transfer the media from one device to another. These processes are managed by software at various levels, to exchange data via Bluetooth, or to mount a media card and read data from it, and of course ultimately software to play back those files. One needs a device such as a cell phone, but not a connection to the internet. In the case of streaming, an internet connection is very much needed, a great deal of data is being extracted, and we never get to own that recording in a format we can share, as we might with an mp4 file. We exchange choice and convenience for data mining. David Arditi argues that this is a feature of modern music capitalism, part of a digital trap leading to unending consumption (Arditi 2018, 2019, 2021).

An important feature of the application of these technologies is that websites often mediate these underlying processes. Although in its earliest days, the code behind web pages was passive markup indicating formatting and linking, the web-based platforms we use every day are active, complex platforms of code working dynamically and connecting numerous entities.

This quotidian aggregation of micro-dynamism results in society being shaped by such platforms; indeed the platforms are part of society. As Dijck (2018) expresses it:

> Platforms, in our view, do not cause a revolution; instead, they are gradually infiltrating in, and converging with, the (offline, legacy) institutions and practices through which democratic societies are organized. That is why we prefer the term "platform society"—a term that emphasizes the inextricable relation between online platforms and societal structures. Platforms do not reflect the social: they *produce* the social structures we live in. . . . (2)

And further, linked to this: "Platforms are neither neutral nor value-free constructs; they come with specific norms and values inscribed in their architectures. These norms may or may not clash with values engraved in the social strictures in which platforms vie to become (or are already) implemented" (2).

Data gets collected, information is extracted from it, sometimes our machines listen for voice commands or musical patterns, and this is aggregated. Whether we search for, then listen to music on a streaming service, or check out some music using a recognition service, we interact with code based technologies that have been shaped by people with particular values and priorities. This will require attention to a number of matters around diversity, power concentration, commerce, ethics, and agency. Smartphones are currently the main source of data collection, and this is now examined.

DATA: COLLECT, LISTEN, EXTRACT, AGGREGATE

There is a long and important historical connection between music and telecommunications technology, and Sterne (2012) explores this while detailing the development and importance of the compact digital file format and encoding process known as mp3. Here I want to focus on smartphones as computing devices rather than phones. They are computers that can also operate as phones, rather than being phones with additional capabilities.[2] Smartphones have several traits that have important implications for the future of music. From a hardware perspective smartphones are all remarkably uniform. While advertisers might spin hype around handset diversity and unique features, the physical differences are marginal. Almost all smartphones have similar dimensions in that they can be held in one hand, they are rectangular, they have a few buttons, a screen, built in cameras, and a headphone socket. With smartphones, diversity of function lies in software, not hardware. Secondly, smartphones tie users to a multinational commerce of advertising driven by metadata collection. The most mundane, everyday acts of musical activity such as sharing have entered this domain. Finally, the way apps are distributed involves a particularly direct connection between users and developers through the specific ecosystems—app stores and associated developer portals—that have emerged.

Although there are millions of apps, there are only really two dominant players in the underlying operating system software on which they are built. By far the most widespread of these is Android, at about 73% of smartphones worldwide, with iOS (Apple) at about 27% ("Mobile Operating System Market Share Worldwide" 2022). While iOS might have more than 50% of the market in the US, UK, and other nations in the Global North, by far the most dominant platform globally, and especially the Global South, is Android. In India, for example, Android has 94% market share. In 2017 Android overtook Windows as the leading operating system as measured by web traffic (Kobie 2017). Although there are numerous companies making phones, only Apple builds devices for the proprietary, closed source iOS operating system (which it also develops), while many companies build phones for the Android operating system. Although Android is open source, Google drives and controls its development. Smartphones are a recent and significant part of the history of computing and digitization (Ceruzzi 2013), and as a result tend to be used more for a much wider range of applications than phone communication.

What kinds of musical activities are people actually undertaking on smartphones and how do we go about exploring the details of this? Compare, for instance, the unambiguous gestures of someone performing on a musical instrument, with the private, small gestures when interacting with a phone. At the sonic level, smartphones widely involve the use of headphones, so even the fundamental aspect of listening as part of performance and musical analysis becomes more difficult. Techniques from digital ethnography will need to become everyday methodological tools in music scholarship here. This will also need to be combined with a more detailed examination of code, algorithms, and discussion of what that code allows, changes, and contributes to communication. Data collection tools known as "analytics" might also need to be harnessed for research purposes.

Although listening is one of the most common activities carried out on smartphones, extending from a longer tradition of portable devices such as the mp3 player and earlier cell phones, the range of capabilities that the proliferation of smartphone apps has enabled is extraordinary. Consider the early 2014 advertisement for the iPhone 5s where the devices are used for all manner of recording and media manipulation, but never as a phone. The advertisement starts with the catchphrase "You're even more powerful than you think" as we see a guitarist on a subway platform with an iPhone connected to his instrument as a virtual effects pedal. Next is an artist with an iPhone strapped to her right hand, tentatively pressing buttons on a synth app, before cutting to a double bass player—the only obviously professional musician so far—using a tuner app. Then we see a young drummer using the phone as a recording device and he starts playing along with the bass, although not particularly in time. This then cuts to a singer singing the synth melody previously played, assisted by a pitch correction app. The groove then picks up; the guitarist joins in and we see someone using the phone to control the lights of a dance performance with our developing ensemble somehow providing the music being danced to. Then the ensemble is a garage band, led by the pitch corrected singer in full swing. The groove tightens again and transforms into a professional sounding cover of *Gigantic* by the Pixies. This then carries on as background music while the ad demonstrates the phone as gaming device, camera, translator, heart rate monitor, model rocket launcher, and mobile planetarium. At no stage is the iPhone being used as a telephone or for passive music listening. The ad focuses on the idea of collaborative music making and values process over material expression. This hyperbolic assertion of personal empowerment—from rank amateurs to professional band in minutes, all with a few apps and a bit of collaboration—might be seen, following Mosco (2005), as a myth of the digital sublime, little more than marketing boosterism of the digerati. Bird (2011), after all, reminds us that most people are still primarily consuming music passively. The hyperbole and exaggeration, however, is based on some actual musical capabilities of a number of apps, extending from a longer history of mobile music computing.

Electronic and art music composers have experimented with cell phones as devices for participation from the early 21st century, and some of the ideas in these approaches around mass participation from around the world have some obvious resonances and opportunities for ethnomusicological discussion (Wang 2014; Wang et al. 2015; Gaye et al. 2006). In universities, cell phone orchestras have been a logical extension from laptop orchestras, and this has been a source of innovative technical and artistic development (Oh et al. 2010; Wang, Essl, and Penttinen 2014). While there are numerous studies exploring the details of algorithms, approaches to coding, limitations of devices and so on (Dahl and Wang 2010; Brian et al. 2010; Tanaka 2004, 2014), the focus tends to be technical, and they do not consider socio-cultural contexts and matters that might arise around perspective, access, representation and power.

While producing music using iPads and iPhones has been possible for some time, a significant part of this has been game-like apps for phones with mass music making participation as a principal aim (Wang et al. 2009). More recently, however, the work of producer Steven Lacy on the 2017 Kendrick Lamar album *Damn* has brought the activity into more mainstream, public view. Lacy essentially produced various elements of the album entirely on his iPhone (Pierce 2017). The video from this story specifically points out how Lacy is sitting in a studio full of expensive equipment, that he does not actually use at all. A point worth making for the Global South impact of this, where access to musical equipment is more difficult, is that the operating system Android is much less capable, at the moment anyway, for music applications. This is due to music production requiring quite low audio latency performance.[3] Tracing this back, audio latency was simply not a high priority when Android was designed, indicating the significance of early design decisions and their long-lasting effects.

We appear to be easily swayed to exchange our data for access to a free service. While an app developer aggregates data about a particular app, ostensibly with the purpose of being able to improve the app and earn more money, corporations aggregating the data of thousands of different music apps represent a highly centralized concentration of power. One of the key ideas behind the model many if not most startups operate under is that there is considerable uncertainty around whether they will work, and if they do, where income will be generated. Large corporations such as Twitter who are losing money, but are still being funded demonstrate this.[4] Under conditions of sectorial transformation, the startup model is a central part of the way modern music commerce operates.

With this in mind, a code musicology needs to ask where value lies, or is seen to lie, for music. At the moment, that is clearly seen as being data. A specific example of this is the online approach to audio mastering by the startup LANDR. Users subscribe to the service, and upload tracks to be mastered. Mastering consists of audio processing including compression, stereo image management, equalization, and reverb, applied subtly to improve the relative loudness of tracks, consistency across a number of different tracks, and what is often described as a sense of polish. Mastering has traditionally been an expensive process undertaken by specialist engineers in specialized studios. LANDR's approach is to add user uploaded tracks to a growing database of tracks, and apply mastering using algorithms developed from machine learning from that database. The more tracks that are uploaded, the bigger their database, and the more information can be extracted and refined, and the better the quality of mastering gets, or so goes the theory. The process of extracting useful information from recorded music is essentially code focused, and will therefore be an important topic in a code musicology of the future.

Once data is collected, information is extracted. This is straightforward in the case of data that has metadata associated with it. Extraction of information is a simple process of collecting text and adding it to a database. Music as digitized audio is more complex to extract information from, and the field of Music Information Retrieval (MIR) has blossomed to solve the complex array of problems involved. Dixon, Gómez, and Volk (2018) point out how although the field is widely known as Music Information Retrieval, many involved tend to think of it as research rather than retrieval, or even use the term "music informatics" (1). A range of analysis techniques, including machine learning and AI are used to retrieve information about rhythmic and timbral features, tempo, and so on. However, the retrieval, collection, and exploitation of the data retrieved is central to the commercial models of the large corporations such as Google and Spotify.

Shazam is a good example of an app being developed by a skilled researcher to help people automatically recognize music they were listening to, which is then transformed by commercial interests who shift it from an open source model to one aimed at getting people to buy music that they have sought information about. The story is mapped out by Razlogiva (2018) who concludes:

> By corporate standards, Shazam has become an app juggernaut. It has over a billion downloads, it has a number of partnerships with major online services, and it integrates with mobile operating systems. Its user data plays a key role in music production decisions. Yet several important groups have interpreted the app's story as decline: open-source software developers; avant-garde musicians and DJs; active app users; as well as hardcore fans of experimental, out-of-print, and non-Western music. They discern a decay of the app's original purpose: loss of serendipity, user agency, and experimentation. For these observers, Shazam's chronology represents the ways corporate digital economies have encroached upon the spheres where open-source software and gray music circulate. (264)

This idea of its data being used for music production decisions is interesting. A person gets a machine to listen and provide information about a track they are unable to identify. If that track is in a particular database of spectral peak patterns then the user gets the information they are after. At the same time, Shazam collects millions of such data points, sells them to other parties for their own use—even for helping to make decisions in the production process. One of the developments here is around the idea of machine listening, privacy, and what this might mean for music in the future.

I interviewed an audio/DSP software engineer at Dolby—Glenn Dickins—and he raised an interesting point about machine listening and data extraction. If a phone responds to a command such as "Hello assistant," it is essentially monitoring all of the audio activity it can capture, and is constantly checking to match what it "hears" with the commands it has been trained to act on. The words we use to describe these devices—hear, respond, trained—have a distinct anthropomorphic aspect, reinforced by the synthesized voices that reply, of course. If our smart speaker sitting in our lounge room is on, waiting diligently for us to ask it to turn the lights on, what does it mean, if anything, as we go about our aural lives and have this device constantly listening? Is that word even applicable to machines?

A couple of years ago, our family bought a car that has the ability to connect a phone and deliver instructions using Google's Android Auto. This involved adjusting the settings on my phone, enabling permissions for location, searching messages and contacts, and so on. For several months I used this whenever I was driving, as it seemed quite convenient, and was certainly, at the time at least, novel. One evening, at home, while checking through my Google account, I came across my search history, and recall being quite astonished at just how much I had searched, and the level of detail that had been retained. Among these were recordings of voice searches that I could play back. I found it distinctly unsettling to hear my voice, that of my 8-year-old son, and background car noise as we made a request to hear some Justin Bieber. It certainly felt like we had been listened to, perhaps because the audio had been recorded. Something had listened, responded, remembered, and then recalled. I subsequently abandoned this type of searching and tightened up my privacy settings.

Who or what is listening here and is that even a word that makes sense for machines? Machine listening is a phrase that has been in use for computing since at least 1992 (Rowe 1992; Collins 2007). Human listening involves some sort of attention and comprehension. In the machine version, the closest parallels lie in the operations underway as a result of running code. The idea of "listeners" in code is quite widespread, in fact, and goes well beyond the idea of sound. A block of code monitors something, and responds to whatever conditions it has been programmed to "hear." A patent for the type of listening Dickins refers to above can be thought of as "trigger listening" (Carreras and Ganeshkumar 2018), in that a particular sound or word is actively listened for, and the device is woken up to listen to a longer search phrase, or whatever happens to be sonically present after that point. It is continuously running code, rather than a microphone, that is doing the listening, as that is the domain in which some sort of comprehension occurs. The ubiquity of such listening through smartphones demands that a code musicology address and refine ideas about machine listening through a focus on the code processes that enable it.

This type of smartphone and smart speaker listening generates a great deal of data, and is held in the most significant quantities by corporations such as Google, Amazon, and Apple. If aggregation in the hands of single corporations offers considerable opportunities for exploitation of metadata, then a raft of concerns will emerge if connections become made between different bodies of data, and between people involved in different musical activities and industries. We are yet to fully understand the effects and implications that cross-linking data, along with identity information, might have. People working with such data imagine, and could certainly implement, ideas that will almost certainly change more mainstream ideas about future possibilities. Discussing data collection by streaming services, then CEO of media education organization Real Industry, Jay LeBoeuf, gave a quick off the cuff example that struck me as questioning some fundamental ideas we have normalized about recordings and their stability. He imagined a scenario where a streaming service could share particular metadata collected about artist tracks. If, for example, a particular threshold of people were shown to click on to another track after a particular period of time (coinciding with a particular song section, for example) that might allow an artist to then modify that track to try and fix this particular metric. Indeed, automating this might even be the next stage. Certainly, work has been done suggesting that streaming services have generally changed the structure of popular music—tracks become shorter and choruses arrive earlier (Kopf 2019). Despite the potential such data might have to transform music and associated activities, at the moment its primary function is to help generate income from advertising.

Although it is not music specific, I want to illustrate this with an experience using Facebook. To promote my app Twotrack, I decided to buy some space in people's feeds through the business component of the site. As an advertising customer, effectively, the interface provides fine grained access to populations organized by interest, gender, age, and location. As I added various filters to target an audience, the interface suggested that, for a few dollars more, I could place ads to many thousands of more people in various places. Facebook sells me access to their data so I can get more people downloading my free app that generates income by itself generating advertising that in turn is controlled by Google. By being music app developers, and music app users, we are tightly tied to the online advertising industries.

Recorded music and advertising has a long history of course, as Taylor (2012) details. Radio, in particular has long understood the need to sell an audience to advertisers, with the musical content as a kind of conduit for this (52). Audience measurement has also long been important (Taylor

2012, 181), and the kind of data available to startups and social media sites is detailed, often realtime, and connectable to other areas of digital life. Streaming services and social media are perhaps best viewed in relation to broadcasting histories, with a key difference being both the specificity and magnitude of the data involved.

While Taylor (2012, 8) so clearly articulates how the sounds of capitalism are everywhere, what we are seeing here is that the most mundane acts of personal musical activity, irrespective of how they sound are also deeply tied to capitalism. The sectorial transformation of the kind being posited here is from the sale of content creation to the creation of data for the advertising industry, all of course now driven by software.

As the data collected becomes more global and diverse, we should be aware of the kind of information that can be collected, and indeed the kinds of influences that researcher and corporation background, context, and associated assumptions might have. Will it be the case that the drive for more diverse data sets ends up coming from companies like Facebook looking to improve their income from the Global South, rather than researchers with more ethical goals in mind? The field of MIR, for example, has recognized a need for more diverse approaches to data collection and takes ethics and diversity seriously, as shown by an article in its inaugural journal issue where they reflect on WEIRD dominance, and ethical responsibilities (Holzapfel, Sturm, and Coeckelbergh 2018).

Important resources for research in MIR lies in particular databases and batches of data, which are often freely available for analysis. Google, for example, offer a data set based on YouTube data (AudioSet, n.d.). How representative of the world's music are the categories in such a set and "ontologies" so created and developed here? Other sets have even more limited origins and stylistic span, begging the question as to whether the tonal pop/rock that dominates the listening world of white male software engineers in San Francisco could unwittingly have a much broader effect on the world's music as such tools are distributed globally? Razlogiva (2018) certainly points out how Shazam is of limited use for African repertoire: "At a closer look, however, Shazam seeks out not music cultures but paying customers. While a wealthy global diaspora may have led Shazam to incorporate South Asian music genres, most African music scenes remain outside of its purview" (261).

So no matter how good the algorithms, and no matter how effective across different kinds of music ultimately is is the deals that are done that matter. Further, the state of big music reveals significant power imbalances that are magnified when we consider scenarios beyond the common Global North.

GLOBAL SOUTH HISTORIES OF TECHNOLOGY

Although Global North experiences of commerce, copyright, genre, and associated practices tend to dominate narratives about music in general, these are by no means universal. It is therefore valuable to consider different histories of music technology and industry in the Global South. This is important in situations where many of the first direct experiences people have with music mediated by software is through smartphones, and when the first use of the internet is also through such devices. When places are considered where these histories are different, a number of challenges for musical diversity, access, relative power, and privacy emerge, and these are particularly tense in situations where public institutions, national infrastructure, legal systems, and protections for freedom of speech and expression are lacking. It will be shown how a code musicology can deepen analysis and offer solutions to emerging problems these contextual differences reveal.

Cell phones have made significant differences in the way people lead their lives. Broader studies about the effects on culture and society of cell phones have demonstrated this, including Goggin (2006) and numerous studies from anthropology which explore topics from health to relationships to communication with spirit worlds centered on the cell phone (Vaarzon-Morel 2014; Telban and Vávrová 2014; Andersen 2013). The use of ringtones as personalized media, the politics involved in their expressive use, and the rise and fall of associated commerce has also been explored (Gopinath 2013, 2005; Padios 2014). The range of experiences is considerable, and the area of focus of most of my ethnomusicological research into music and technology, Papua New Guinea, is an excellent example. This is an area ideally suited to analysis of diversity and rapid social and technological change, so I will draw on it for examples of changes that cell phone and smartphone use has wrought there.

In Papua New Guinea, smartphones extend a slightly longer history (since 2007) of cell phones being used to share mp3 files via Bluetooth and exchange of SD cards. For the growing number of smartphone users, these devices are often the first sustained personal experience of the internet; indeed for many it is the first real engagement with computing more generally. Data is relatively expensive and although social media activity is widespread, sharing of media via these sites is not extensive at all. Audio and video simply use too much data for average users in Papua New Guinea given existing prices. A contested, not particularly lucrative system of cassette royalty payments (not copyright based) has given way to no real form of income for musicians other than direct sales of their recording before the files are copied and distributed digitally.

With this in mind, it is useful to compare developments in music more broadly from pre-cell phone to post-cell phone in Melanesia with the Global North:

Melanesia	Global North
From cassettes to digital files	From mp3 files to streaming
No internet to phone internet	Home and work internet to phone internet
No computer to phone computer	Desktop computing to phone computing
more project studios; fewer large studios	Similar

There is a more gradual, stepped nature of technological change widely experienced in the Global North and events occur slightly earlier. An example from my own area of research has shown that musicians, who were making small incomes from cassette sales rapidly had this recording-based income cut almost completely with the introduction of cell phones. Change like this can then be seen as a relentless, intrusive commodification that, as yet, does not provide enough opportunity for musicians to make money to buy the commodities needed to create, share, and discuss music. What is common with most of these local narratives is the connection to transnational commerce in the form of Google through Android phones.

The flexibility that digital sharing enables challenges content creators in that it is harder to make money from that content. That is important because money is needed; consumption is required to even be involved at all in the most mundane of musical activities—listening, sharing, and discussing. Most people in Papua New Guinea do not have waged employment, and where they do it is relatively low. The result is that while musicians need to obtain expensive devices (laptops, phones) to make, share, and listen to music, they are not making any income from the content they are providing. Seen from this perspective, this end of the consumption economy, the imbalance, unfairness, and challenges for music become more obvious.

If shifts in the nature of music commodification have introduced a new set of economic tensions, then that becomes entwined with social justice issues when we turn to places where data collection has potentially more sinister implications that could lead to arrest, imprisonment, or worse. Protest songs, for example, can be transformed from locally bound expressions of opinion and resistance, to something more easily monitored (and monetized) by the very organizations and governments likely to be targets of such protest. This occurs simply through the digital channels being used (YouTube, for example) and how the corporate owners exercise their growing power and relationship to governments.

Although the kinds of changes underway in Papua New Guinea are quite extensive and compressed into a short time span, the point is there is quite a different history of music technology and related commerce. Other Global South areas also have different histories, and that is the key point. While loss of royalty income has been a result of technology corporations such as Google and Apple becoming involved in music distribution, in places where royalty income has never really operated at all (China and many parts of Africa, for example) the change is obviously different in nature and significance.

Such differences in experiences of change occur in other domains, of course, including telecommunications, computing, and electricity. For vast numbers of people, landlines have never been present in anything other than main urban areas, so first experiences of telecommunications are with cell phones. Similarly, the first regular personal computing occurs with smartphones. Many villages in Papua New Guinea have never had grid supplied electricity, and now rely exclusively on solar power. Development is not a linear process following patterns experienced by the Global North and experiences of change cannot simply be translated elsewhere. This is a problem of perspective and experience and is exacerbated by the overwhelmingly Global North bias in musicological scholarship.

The appification of musical activity and the growth of cell phone infrastructure in the Global South, along with concomitant increases in mobile internet access means that these issues of power have more significant global effects. Concentration of power into large corporations centered in the Global North raises concerns about technological colonialism, if not imperialism. What does it mean when control over massive amounts of once social and participatory content is in the hands of relatively few very large, powerful transnational corporations? Is the convenience of corporate social media sites worth paying for with our data, and the sort of surveillance, and threats to privacy and diversity that ensue? This can too easily be seen as benign, particularly in Global North worlds where incomes are high, legal systems function fairly, and infrastructure such as electricity, access to water, shelter, health services, and so on are taken for granted, the situation is more fraught and loaded elsewhere, where such things might well be the exception than the norm.

NOTES

1. For more on music, copying, and analog to digital continuity see Borschke (2017).

2. Software was also crucial to the operation of older cell phones. *Symbian* was the operating system of most Nokia phones, for example.

3. Audio latency is the time gap between the input of a signal and its output after going through conversion and processing in the digital domain in the device.

4. See, for example, Volz and Mukherjee (2016).

Conclusion

I will now muster key ideas from previous chapters under a series of tenets to codify our code musicology. The tenets cover a wide span of music and music related topics, and their effects can be diverse. To help connect these wide-ranging ideas I draw on an important observation from Kitchin and Dodge (2011) about conditions being *modulated* by code. This has a particularly apt musical analog and provides a valuable explanation of how the effects of code and associated infrastructure play out in musical domains. I then map out some strategies to apply this style of musicology to help navigate the ongoing, at times rapid musical change not always driven by obviously musical phenomena.

MODULATION

In an attempt to broadly characterize or speak about the effects of code and its widespread effects and complexity, Kitchin and Dodge (2011) offer the idea of modulation: "one of the primary reasons why software makes a difference to the world people inhabit is because *it modulates the conditions under which sociospatial processes operate*" (Kitchin and Dodge 2011, 65) (emphasis in original).

They posit that the pervasiveness of code "now conditions existence in the West—code is routinely embedded into everyday objects, infrastructures, and systems" (260) and go so far as to suggest that "it is impossible to now live outside of its orbit" (260). They add that this need not be direct, in that we can engage with code and its effects at a distance. They are focused on how spaces come into being and are partly defined and transformed by the technicity of code in operation. Music, as a phenomenon unfolding in time and space is an ideal example of the sort of code/space they describe. If one is listening to music that has been created through the operation of code somehow, as is increasingly the case, then one is engaging at some level with how that code has modulated the conditions under which that music has been created, distributed. and the space and time in which it occurs.

Why not simply mediation? Partly because of the sometimes unpredictable results that occur when the agency of code is involved. I will explore some specific examples shortly, but first some more musical discussion of how modulation is useful. The idea resonated with me, in no small part because I was experimenting with the DAW Bitwig, which has a particularly flexible approach to allowing sonic parameters to be changed periodically by other signals. An example might be a low frequency oscillator, cycling at say once per second, being connected to the volume of another oscillator cycling much faster at an audio rate and being audible as a result. That second oscillator, which we hear as a pitched note, then pulsates in volume based on the first oscillator. This is what modulation refers to in musical production and synth focused discussion. This is a very simple example, but the idea is that modulation is a way of capturing a broad range of effects over a variety of parameters. Layered modulation, where a modulator might modulate another modulator, can lead to highly complex behavior. This is particularly evident when experimenting with modulation possibilities on a synthesizer. It is also a useful conceptual device to think about how code operates. The next section uses this idea over a number of important topics that have emerged, and attempts to explain this through a number of examples.

CODING VALUES

Values get coded, and culture can lie in code as much as in other texts. As a result, reading code and exploring its creation can be a useful source of material for analysis.

Earlier chapters showed how musical values get coded. The rise of digital emulation to re-create sounds of vintage analog gear such as tube guitar amplifiers and studio equipment shows how valued aesthetics and approaches to workflow are maintained. This extends further to the emulation in software of obsolete digital hardware so that sounds of synths such as the DX-7 can be used by people without having vintage equipment.

There are less direct examples as well. People who write code have experiences, understanding and values that can also directly influence the constraints and affordances that make certain musical practices and workflows easier than others. Bates (2016), in exploring how DAWs are used in studios in Turkey posits the idea of "digital tradition." He points out that: "Various technologies are incorporated into preexisting labor contexts and social norms in surprising ways, which has implications for both our understanding of what precisely these technologies enable and what these technologies are" (354).

These tools of such digital tradition are built from code, by people, and a code musicology should be an important part of seeking such understanding.

TIME

It is important for a code musicology to explore digital rendering of musical time, as that is where fundamental ideas we have about music are re-created but also challenged and modified.

A code musicology will need to explore changing relationships between sequence, repetition and variation as the code-based aspect of our digital media affords change in that domain as much as it affords consistency. Thinking about time provides an excellent first example of code modulating music when thought of as a set of sociospatial processes. For this discussion, what is important is that music proceeds sequentially in time, an idea so obvious as to appear facile, until the nature of how time is organized digitally enters the discussion. In an analog environment, thinking back here to the example from Chapter 3 and the instantaneous nature of an analog electrical circuit, time did not have to be managed. The very existence of the idea of digital realtime exposes significant differences between the digital and analog domains. We can think of code essentially freezing time for a moment, operating on single chunks of data in bursts that are fed to a buffer before conversion to the analog domain to a form our human perception systems can interpret.

The historical moment of realtime combining with random access storage tends to be a technical feature lost among other developments, but it marks a critical conceptual moment for music. Several layers of code and additional digital data working out how to put it all back together are required for reconstitution in our musically expected time order. Once we conceptualize and think about that space—or period of time really—where code is piecing things back into order then not only do we see an obvious example of code modulating conditions under which processes operate, but some deeper fundamental, indexical relationships that have been normalized for recorded music are called into question. Wendy Chun has put forth some useful parallel observations from photography, which will help illustrate these ideas more clearly.

Chun (2011, 15) points out how the onset of digital photography brought forth anxiety about the future of photography as the indexical link between film as artifact and image was challenged. Two key features are at play in this anxiety; firstly the contrast between the relative stability of photography and the ease of manipulation fundamental to an image in the digital domain. Images can be manipulated more readily and so the "truth" of image as representing the real becomes fluid, at play, and under test. Secondly, is the relative ease with which such digital data can be copied compared to photographs as physical pieces of paper. As more and more images circulate because they can be trivially copied and manipulated any singular indexical authority is challenged. While some direct parallels can be made here with music around the ease of manipulation and copying, there is another indexical link I want to explore.

One of the important concepts for late 20th century thinking about recording, from R. Murray Schafer, is the notion of schizophonia, where in the case of recordings, sound becomes split from its source. Recordings broke the once indexical relation between source and sound. Records, tape, and CDs indexically link the sequence in which something was recorded to its output from the recording. The sequence of a performance equals the sequence in which we hear it from the recording. Tape challenged that relation, but only so far as greater ease of manipulation; tape could be played backwards, it could be chopped up and re-arranged. There were physical limits to this as well, as one could only chop up tape, splice, and re-splice a certain number of times. It also involved specialized equipment and skills so was not widely accessible.

The indexical relationship between physical sequence on the media and musical sequence in time was broken from the moment sound was represented digitally by being stored on media non-sequentially. Code is vested with a particular kind of agency so that decisions might be made to play things back in a different order, or with repetition. It is worth re-iterating a comment made earlier that in a digital non-sequential mode of storage it is just as easy to play something back in chronological order as it is in some other order. One has no affordance advantage over the other as a fundamental property of its mediality.

This obviously accords strongly with those positing that digitally produced musics tend to highlight extensive modification in the time domain—looping, reversing, cutting, and so on. We have forms that have grown out of recorded music traditions, and we build musical tools that re-create fundamental values and features of that music history (listening from a beginning to an end, for example!) but this is not a quality inherent in the media. As such indexical links break, repetition and sequence are highly likely candidates for significant change potential in future music making. In a sense, the idea of code agency here is more akin to notions of human improvisation in music. I certainly do not want to suggest (yet, anyway) that machine decision making is directly comparable from an aesthetic point of view to human musical improvisation, but there are important conceptual similarities.

Earlier analog recording technology such as the phonograph and tape precluded easy manipulation in time, or at least tended to render the range of possible transformation types as relatively limited. A great deal more can be done, and faster, with digital audio in the time domain, thus fostering style change as musicians explore such capabilities. The painstaking work behind compositions exploring the potential of tape splicing and rejoining by avant garde composers later became an everyday act for a much wider range of musicians. That wider use results in a proliferation of new styles and genres that affect and influence a much wider span of the human population. Again, these transformations have taken place not merely due to digitization, but through the operation of code. The digitization is a necessary condition in providing data for that code to operate on.

While these ideas are conjectural in thinking about a future, there are examples of music currently being made that do exhibit exploration of the time domain in novel ways, and in the case here, the very idea of a singular musical sonic text is at play. Rebekah Wilson has been experimenting with a form of collaborative music making that places network latency—usually regarded as an impediment to musical communication—at the center.[1] Wilson has coded what she calls a score that coordinates performers connected via the internet but that does so with the delay caused by latency as a key structural element in the music so created. There are two or more sides to this performance; each performer in a different location hears a different result. There is no single sonic text here. There is interaction, collaboration, aesthetic choice, response, and pleasure from the interpretation, however. To demonstrate the idea with familiar repertoire, Wilson shows a slide of a Bach chorale, as it was composed, and then as if each part was delayed in relation to the other (as might happen with latency) and then pieced back together. Wilson has written code that actively modulates conditions through syncing, quantizing, incorporating latency and thus assisting in creating music with built in out-of-phase relationships. There is a score, which is in the form of code, instructions, and two networked performers at a distance. This is described as music that is "latency native," a music born with latency. Latency is not going to go away in a networked digital environment in the near future, so she explores ways of making music with others with the latency as an integral part of the creative process.

CODE CAN CHANGE WHAT MUSIC CAN BE

Code not designed for an obviously musical context or purpose can have musical consequences.

While many of the examples explored previously had specifically musical aims in mind, that is not always the case. Any computer user is aware of the occasional unintended consequences of software, and this in turn can have sonic and musical consequences.

The affordances and constraints that coders navigate and create offer expanded possibilities for musical futures and innovative artists explore these. Latency native performances and the resulting different sonic results depending on audience/performer perspective offer phase relationships so far not encountered in musical ensemble performance. "Corposing" plays with time scales that would be completely unmanageable without a computing environment at the center of their creation and rendering. The practices of live coding and the tools used question preconceived ideas of the separation between performer, instruments, and score.

COMPLEX ACTION BEHIND SIMPLE ACTIVITIES

Fundamental to a code musicology at this particular historical juncture is recognizing and exposing the politics and effects of complex hidden actions behind mundane, quotidian musical activities.

A valuable, guiding observation is to recognize that increasingly, our mundane musical activities such as listening invoke complex connections, flows of data and ties to transnational IT and advertising commerce dominated by a few massive corporations. Because of its reach, it is a complexity that should not be ignored.

GLOBAL CODE IS MOBILE CODE

The logic and global spread of appification and associated commerce form important parts of code musicology.

The increasingly global reach of code and its modulation of music, surrounding activities, and wider cultural context is smartphone centered. The reach of my own simple app demonstrates this. Google's push, along with other corporations such as Facebook into Global South markets reinforces the momentum of this phenomena. The pervasiveness of code globally is largely due to the rise of computing on smartphones, and how this has changed the reach and nature of software development more broadly. As Morris and Elkins (2015) note ". . . we define app as a moment in the history of the software commodity when the form, distribution model and economics behind software production have shifted to encourage a proliferation of mundane software and an intensified integration of software into everyday routines" (70).

To become widely used means being free or of very low cost, expanding reach to enable commodification of mundane acts through data collection: "Free apps set the ground for freemium models (where the initial download is free and extra services/features are purchased), and even apps that remain free for the duration of their use rely on data collection, advertising and other very non-free forms of surveillance and monitoring (Andrejevic 2013)" (Morris and Elkins 2015, 76).

This is part of the appification of music. The personal costs of appification and the proliferation of free and freemium apps lies in needing to be a consumer of smartphones and telecommunications services to take part in providing masses of personal information to drive advertising revenue to huge corporations whose power and earning potential increases as that data becomes more detailed.

INDUSTRY

A code musicology will inevitably need to attend to matters that are dominant and important in this code centered industry, including privacy, machine listening and MIR.

A code musicology relies on understanding code focused commercial frameworks involving data collection, machine listening, and advertising. Throughout the book, the thread of transectorial innovation has been evident, working incrementally to the stage where I have argued that the term sectorial transformation is more apt. The rise of code as a critical mediator and modulator is at the center of this. Enabling that rise, interestingly, was the widespread incorporation of the CDROM into consumer computers, as it allowed data to be transferred to hard drives and related forms of computing storage. This marked a Trojan horse moment, as Morris (2015, 35–36) points out. It is somewhat ironic that the CD, a format that revived physical media sales for the music industries of the Global North provided the point of transition to computer-based media. Once in those forms and easily transferable via networks an industry that had been based on shifting physical products had to adapt rapidly.

It is the movement to smartphones, their ubiquity, virtually constant network connection and the idea of appification that marks a more final point in this sectorial transition. Associated with this has been the shifting of the commercial model, the way things are "monetized" to models characteristic of IT startups and corporations more broadly. The smartphone is an extraordinary collector of data, and that lies at the core of the commerce of appification; advertising is the main business. The service based streaming industries, by ensuring that an internet connection is essential, generate revenue through data aggregation from millions of micro-transactions.

As a result of this sectorial shift, music industries are subservient to, or dominated by IT industries. A better way to think about this is that music industries are now largely part of the IT industries. With a code musicology, then, things that matter or have significance in these code-based industries are likely to exert influence or have significance for music and associated activities, and should therefore be a focus of analysis.

PRIVACY

Vast quantities of data are being collected about the listening habits and other musical activities of people globally. The implications of this should be examined by a code musicology

One such broader concern in society around corporations like Facebook and Google is that of privacy, and these are increasingly carrying over to musical activities. While writing this, I read a report describing a patent recently granted to Spotify titled "Identification of taste attributes from an audio signal" (Hulaud 2018). It describes a proposed system where both speech content and background noise could be listened to, metadata gathered, and music or other content delivered based on analysis of this audio. The patent states that this analysis might include extraction of metadata about emotional state, gender, age, accent, aspects of physical environment, and number of people. Listening suggestions could also include consideration of historical preferences of a listener, or preferences of friends of a user.

This is a patent, and not yet something actually being used, but there is some chance that it could be. The transnational nature of such corporations raises challenges for and complications for laws around protection of privacy. As computer security and privacy expert Schneier points out, in the US, privacy is not particularly well protected through legislation, as say, in Europe.

Europe has more stringent privacy regulations than the United States. In general, Americans tend to mistrust government and trust corporations. Europeans tend to trust government and mistrust corporations. The result is that there are more controls over government surveillance in the U.S. than in Europe. On the other hand, Europe constrains its corporations to a much greater degree than the U.S. does. U.S. law has a hands-off way of treating internet companies. Computerized systems, for example, are exempt from many normal product-liability laws. This was originally done out of the fear of stifling innovation. (Mineo 2017)

Spotify is a Swedish company, and the patent is in the US. Notice also how the Global South is just not part of this discussion at all, that should be of concern, as the effects of these matters could certainly span a wider range in circumstances where States and Governments might be ineffective, corrupt, over-reaching, imposing martial law, and so on.

When code has been created, supported, and used by powerful corporations the choice of language, libraries, and operating system can modulate music and have long-term effects. Consider the following two examples, one characterized by likely inattention or lack of priority to particular technical details and the other more strategic, but both with long term, widespread, even global effects for music.

Commercial and technical decisions made at the beginning of the Android smartphone era have had repercussions for mobile music making since. From 2003, a company called Android Inc. developed the basis of an operating system written in Java originally aimed at digital cameras of the time. Google acquired Android in 2005, worked on the software and released it for phones in 2008. Despite being built on top of the highly audio capable Linux operating system, the underlying architecture of Android was never designed with audio performance in mind. Those decisions, over a decade ago now, have essentially crippled the devices for music production in comparison to the capabilities of its main competitor, Apple's iOS. Now while this might just mean Global North musicians tend to choose Apple devices to make music, the dominance of Android in the Global South makes the global effects of these early decisions particularly unbalanced.

Operating systems do not appear overnight, so those we might be using in a few years time are being developed now. One such example, driven by Google and open source is the Fuchsia operating system (https://fuchsia.dev/). If the history of Android is anything to go by, and Fuchsia becomes widely used, decisions about the audio architecture made now could well be having musical effects globally in a decade from now. A code musicology will need to consider that possibilities for music will be afforded and constrained by quite technical decisions lying deep in nascent code bases today. While Google's approach to open source contributions is a relatively healthy one, it is important to not overstate philanthropic benefits; some decisions appear to be quite strategic, as the Web Audio examples discussed earlier suggested. Having more people connected to the internet while carrying out their musical activities has obvious benefits to a company with a business model built around data collection for advertising.

CODE AS CULTURAL HERITAGE

Code and software contain elements of and affect musical heritage and tradition. A code musicology will need to be concerned with methods to both archive and analyze these elements and effects.

Aspects of our musical heritage now reside in code, and that is highly likely to be the case for some time. That will entail approaches to its collection, archiving, and ability to continue to run it once the hardware it was designed to run on is no longer available. This is especially important in situations where interactivity is a key part of the music; the interactivity is not really possible without the code running. We might end up saving particular instances of music from recordings of a game being played, but ideally the full potential for future research lies in keeping and accessing the code, and playing the game. That will mean careful archiving of old software, and devices or emulators able to run it. This is also where the archival and long term advantages of open source software become obvious. Recall the Csound case, where programs written from 1986 can be rendered today, and something written today should be compatible with future versions of Csound. That is an example of long-term design excellence that no proprietary software has even come close to achieving. Most commercial music software makes money in conservative, traditional ways, of course, so being open source has not been seen as an option. A code musicology should encourage commercial music software creators as to the cultural and historic value of their products. The Sopwith game provides an excellent practical example, in that old source code was released under an open-source license, enabling it to be ported to current devices, while emulating older sound behavior and maintaining the sonic integrity of the original. Retro games demonstrate an interesting tension between the law and archiving cultural heritage. Modern emulations rely on pirated copies of the original ROM chip software. Such games are kept working by users around the world sharing those ROM copies and playing the games on devices such as the Raspberry Pi. Ultimately, however, the practice of collecting those ROMs, due to copyright, is illegal in many if not most places.

There is a related issue in regards to digitized content, and the tendency to regard aspects of sites such as YouTube and Facebook as being useful repositories of shared information. Consider the following example from an ethnomusicological study of singing competitions in Micronesia. Diettrich (2016) describes a singing competition held on Facebook for members of the Micronesian communities; at home and away. These represent modern, vital forms of participation and ways of identifying for such groups. In the discussion, however, we learn that by the time of publication, some of the Facebook pages were no longer available, but videos had been "archived" on YouTube.

We should ask what sort of archiving this is, certainly in relation to that in the sense known by most ethnomusicologists. A particular account holder has uploaded this material. That account holder could remove them anytime; in that sense they have ownership. Google/YouTube will still have that material, however. Of course, if someone or an algorithm believes the material contravenes copyright law, it could be removed too. YouTube has some very specific rules around the use of material it hosts. As a researcher, if I was interested in keeping a copy for myself by downloading the content using one of the many utilities available to do this, and therefore avoiding the problem if the content was removed by the original account holder or YouTube, I would be breaking the terms and conditions. YouTube is becoming a more useful and diverse source of material from all over the world. It feels public, it is free, but it is privately owned, and that free of cost comes at the price of contributing to data to be aggregated for commercial purposes. Diettrich's example clearly demonstrates to me the need for a wider discussion about what these public feeling but actually privately held repositories mean in the longer term.

Open-source programs and music, particularly where the score is released as well, offer much greater potential to survive over long periods of time. Open-source emulations will be useful ways of archiving sonic histories in ways that can be used long after closed source plugins and their ilk fail to work. Companies should be encouraged, and the cultural value demonstrated, of releasing old, unused, or obsolete source code as part of a software museum or vault of cultural heritage.

PACE OF CHANGE

Over the few years of researching and writing this book the pace of change in technological developments and their societal effects has become clearly evident. Research is proceeding rapidly, and Google, in particular, is forging ahead with research on machine learning and music that quickly results in widely available apps and online resources. The ability to hum a tune in to a search engine and have a good chance of getting a sensible result is such an example. The energy that has gone into Web Audio in just a few years is another. This underscores a critical point for a code musicology, which is the need to adapt and respond effectively in a rapidly changing environment. https://research.google/ is an interesting place to get a sense of this more broadly, and we should bear in mind how this research supposedly feeds into Google's overall mission which is "to organise the world's information and make it universally accessible and useful" (https://about.google/). It will be important to keep watching where time and effort is being invested, then asking, for example, why an advertising company would be doing this, and what it might mean for music in all its diversity, and not just that of the Global North? Is it necessarily the case that all cultures will want to have their music universally accessible? This is particularly important when many people have quite different sets of beliefs, practices, and aesthetics around music than those of the Google fraternity.

A CODE MUSICOLOGY MANIFESTO

Since at least 2014, many of the concerns raised so far have been expressed in a *musictechifesto*, authored by a leading scholar of music technology, Jonathan Sterne. This manifesto provides clear, articulate tenets to structure ideal approaches to music technology (Sterne 2014b). This has been endorsed by a long list of academics, musicians, educators, and others interested in music technology. Many concepts that a code perspective on music analysis reveals are addressed in the manifesto. Consider power, cultural perspective, and imbalance, for example:

> Meaningful innovation is sustainable and just—yet the current landscape of music technology favors short-term profit-making, too often at the expense of deeper cultural concerns. . . . Like other cultural workers, many who contribute most to the richness of musical cultures lead increasingly precarious economic lives. But those who stand to profit the most economically have the biggest say in policy discussions. Too often music technologies are used as tools of exclusion rather than inclusion. Because what counts as "music," "technology," and "music technology" is unsettled, those with the most power create the most powerful definitions. (Sterne 2014b)

The manifesto speaks to diversity:

> Meaningful innovation bridges multiple perspectives—yet the music technology field remains predominantly white, male, and tends toward assumptions that its user base is Western and able-bodied. (Sterne 2014b)

The active forward reaching section of the manifesto, under the title "Let's Build Better Worlds," proposes the following:

> Music technologies make worlds. Let us make better worlds. Let music technology do good, serve public interest, foster belonging, justice, collaboration and sharing, enable greater access to positive musical experiences and personal connections, and create durable objects and practices.
> We call for greater awareness of the cultural forces already in new music technologies, and the courage to challenge or change them when the collective good demands it.
> Ask of any music technology: For whom will this make things better? How? Is it open or closed to creativity and innovation it has not yet anticipated?
> Ask of any policy: Whose rights and opportunities are being promoted? Whose are being eroded? What idea of culture does it presume?
> Ask of any practice: Who is invited to join in? Who is left out? Where will it find support?
> Ask of any organization: How does it help people come together? Does it exploit them in doing so? (Sterne 2014b)

Central to this is the idea of widening the scope of agency in the development of music technology, and emphasizing that development should occur in ways that promote inclusiveness, encourage diversity, and affirm individual and collective rights. The "we" referred to in the following quote will increasingly come up against the need to work on these matters through code, and analysis of the processes that code enables:

> Those concerned with music technology must develop a sense of ourselves as a "we" across different fields: creators, theorists, scholars, engineers, journalists, lawyers, activists, policy-makers, and others all together. We may not always agree, but we must have a sense of the whole and of our places within it. We must acknowledge one another as equals so that we can collaborate on equal footing. (Sterne 2014b)

This above quote is something this book speaks to. In arguing for the importance of code for music, combined with the lack of understanding and analysis from music scholars, the aim is to connect the technical, engineering aspects with the cultural. I hesitate to write in such binary terms, as it tends to pre-suppose that the technical can be separated—as though technology exists in a cultural vacuum. How then, might we go about drawing on the work of software studies in musical contexts to better think about future contexts in which code is in operation?

With this in mind, and returning to some of the principles outlined in the ideals expressed in the *musictechifesto*, what opportunities exist for resistance of these trends? Are there better ways to drive music technology under such circumstances? How might agency be recovered for a more direct stake in music technology (beyond advertising at least) as outlined in the *musictechifesto*? To redress some of the concerns around power, diversity, security, and openness we will need to not only understand what is happening more clearly, but how to create software in new ways. That involves a code centered analysis, and an approach to future code development that responds to knowledge and insights so gained. New sites of fieldwork for digital ethnography will need to be identified and explored.

> *Future research in code musicology should involve co-research, interviews, discussion, and checking with the authors of code.*

Sterne has pointed out how imagining better worlds for music can usefully emerge from a critique of the history of music technology (Sterne 2014a, 244). Here, I would like to imagine a world that addresses key problems evident for music around economic and social justice as smartphones more and more shape diverse musical practices. As Schneier has pointed out, free (as in cost) services come at the price of users becoming the product, contributing reams of metadata to be mined for advertising purposes. It will be important to make Global South users very aware of what this means for music in situations of protest, or for music of persecuted minorities, and others in tense political situations. Internet connectivity is at the core of privacy concerns, and because of the obscure, proprietary operation of software, exactly what data is moving where is difficult, if not impossible to determine. Creating code that is open, transparent, and that allows people to see exactly what they are sharing and why, is needed. Projects such as Briar (https://briarproject.org/) have recognized this and offer practical alternatives that meet these criteria of openness. Such work also recognizes the different nature of connectivity in the Global South which is often intermittent and of low bandwidth.

Transectorial innovation from computing demands analysis and understanding in those new industrial domains to actually understand what is happening to music, and how commerce has shifted. That means understanding what is going on in software, as that is the medium that is directly involved in these shifts. Subverting the commercial imperatives of global corporations as they spread to the Global South, or at least finding alternatives that allow local musicians to earn something to be able to participate in a highly commodified musical world will be essential. It will be valuable to explore musician-centric possibilities for earning money from music using tools from the world of computing—the main agents in sectorial transformation—so that different possibilities may be thought through, and different possibilities coded.

The infrastructure put in place for app development allows for hitherto unheard of access to an audience for individual developers, groups, as well as larger businesses and corporations of course. Coder diversity is important, and encouraging people to code from a wider population with more experience of specific musics should be a priority. Open source projects are also highly effective here and if correctly managed, can be inclusive sites for production. Navigating the best kind of code for local musical conditions should be a high priority. It will be necessary to make objects that make sense for diverse musics and musical practices, rather than forcing workarounds as a result of making universal decisions about musical structure. Time signatures built in to many applications, are one such example. The dominance of the keyboard interface could be rapidly challenged in a distributed app environment, with more local instrument interfaces emerging. There are aesthetic priorities and different musical value emphases to be factored in as well.

An important idea that emerges from the development cycle, and that relates to discussions around skeuomorphism explored previously, is that at some point, decisions have to be made about what the universal structuring elements will be (as seen in the *Tone js* MultiPlayer example). That is, what will be made available for use by everybody using that library, and what will be left to developers to implement in their own code? That is an ongoing process leading to better and more useful higher-level code for developers to use. The sooner Global South coders join this, music developers included, the better. It is with such an approach to code that imperatives and tenets in the *musictechifesto* will be best addressed, providing alternatives to approaches solely or at least primarily focused on the collection and sale of metadata for advertising by global corporations.

If problems revealed and indeed partly lie in the nature and operation of software, might the solutions exist in the same domain? One approach might be an applied ethnomusicology of software and app creation associated with whatever the current devices are. As codejects they demand analysis of their code as much as their hardware and putting some of our focus there will be of value. In addition, engagement with the MIR community should be taken more seriously by those more focused on the scholarship of music and culture. Ideally, scholars of music technology should become involved with organizations like the W3C. Once the implementation starts, things become harder to change and steer.

This book has demonstrated how application of an analytical methodology drawing from software studies, critical code studies, and the digital humanities offers insights into power, commerce, and musical possibilities. As we move to a future where software and code continue to exert influences in ever more complicated and integrated ways, this perspective will be critical for music scholars in popular music, ethnomusicology, as well as musicians, and hopefully engineers. If important aspects of musical change and our musical culture will be occurring in the code that we use every day, then more of us will need to read code, change some, write some maybe, criticize it, delete it, fear it even, but above all engage with it.

NOTES

1. See https://latencynative.com.

Appendix 1
Definitions

Algorithm

A particular method to solve a problem or carry out a specific task of varied complexity.

Code

Instructions written or inscribed in a form that can be read by humans.

Codebase

A coherent collection of source code files and configuration files in a repository or collection. Coherency usually means the codebase is for a particular application, group of applications, or code library.

Digitisation

The process of converting an analog signal, such as audio, into a series of numbers in a format that can be interpreted by computing devices.

Digitalisation

The processes involved in moving activities (within a business, for example) from being analog (paper, filing cabinets) to digital (word processed documents, files on a hard drive).

Port

To make changes to a codebase to allow it to run on different devices and/or operating systems.

Software

A catch-all term to describe packages or bundles of instructions in various forms (as code, or as compiled instructions only readable by computers) whether readable by humans or not. It can be used to collect programs together in layers—an operating system software layer, for example. It is the thing one might buy and in material form generally consists of data that has been compiled and packaged.

Appendix 2
Twotrack App Reviews Discussed

Id	Date/time	Rating	Review
1	2014-07-29 T01:52:33Z	5	Jodiah Tip 1 keep screen on, disable sleep modes. Tip 2 disable auto rotate, after that I've had no problems.
2	2016-11-09 T20:14:40Z	3	Im not sure Sometimes it sends the wrong recording through bluetooth idk is some one listening to the recordings
3	2013-08-31 T16:51:47Z	5	Best android multi track. At first the timing of my tracks were way off but luckily I found the settings and fixed it right up, also head phones are a MUST OR IT WONT WORK!
4	2014-01-06 T20:40:26Z	4	Excellent This is everything I wanted in a small easy to use app for experimenting multi tracked singing whenever and wherever an idea hits. Some funky crashes when changing the screen orientation prevented 5 stars though.
5	2014-05-25 T20:00:57Z	5	I just started a band So I jusy started a band and the only thing I have tonrecord on is my tablet, now me and my group are recording professtional sounding tracks off this app so thankyou guys for making it, make sure when you do your second recording tonwear headphones in one ear to know whats goin on
6	2014-12-24 T11:19:56Z	4	Super groovy Its perfect for laying down my guitar tracks so i can sit back and focus on vocals and melody. I love that i have this ability on my flippin electronic cellular multi functional smart phonetically old saggy bewbs.
7	2015-02-28T 11:27:38Z	5	Good for baby :. good for me! Was able to record a soothing 4 track lullaby for our 4 week old son: holding baby in my left arm at the same time . . . impressed!
8	2014-08-13 T01:12:03Z	5	Recruting for six sins I made a band like thing with people who rap anyone wana join?
9	2014-08-20 T20:28:05Z	5	Best App In The World! !!! Made My Raps Using This App!!!

Appendix 2

Id	Date/time	Rating	Review
10	2014-09-22 T05:50:05Z	5	Handier than a pocket on a shirt. Perfect as can be for a free app. Allows me to lay down some lead guitar over rhythm and vocals. The track overlay timing adjustment is the reason you get a 5th star from me. I def recommend this app.
11	2014-12-05 T11:53:28Z	4	Nice app Great way to work out Leads and improvise different scales & modes without firing up your entire studio. Good for harmony practice too! Record a major scale, and harmonize in 2nds–7ths. For lessons, I'm on fiverr under Greg Clagett. I teach advanced so if you haven't been playing 5–10 years, it may be too advanced. I do try to put up intermediate (finger exercises, & drills) lessons once a month.
12	2015-04-25 T23:00:19Z	5	2Track Audio Recorder Who needs to pay for studio time anymore
13	2015-08-15 T02:27:24Z	4	Great app once you adjust latency It takes a lot of trial and error to find the right latency adjustment but, once you do, the app works great. Mine is 140 ms. I use the app to play lead guitar over the rhythm tracks that I record. Love the simple no bs interface too. Very user friendly and easy to share your creations.
14	2015-11-11 T14:44:38Z	4	Coolness For recording simple guitar riffs,ideas etc it suits my purpose brilliantly. The ability to share it straight to my SoundCloud makes it to four stars,I may come back n give it five after testing it more thoroughly but for a first use it's a very simple bit of coolness that doesn't need to see my identity location or contacts, so not a scam like most of these apps usually are. Good work ppl !
15	2016-01-23 T11:13:45Z	4	Not bad for putting down quick guitar lines on a tablet
16	2014-03-30 T06:59:00Z	4	If you import an mp3 on the master track then press record, the overdub will be your voice recording. This is good because I'm a hip hop artist and I need this kind of thing. One problem. After pressing record, the song plays the way it's supposed to. But when I stop it and press play, the overdub is either too late or too early. This throws the rhythm way off. You need to sync the master track with the overdub as soon as the record button is pressed to prevent any delay. Please fix then I will give 5 stars.
17	2014-01-01 T17:32:40Z	3	Great but sync issues The sound quality is superb and the app is very easy to use. Perfect for song writing or just playing around with ideas. Only issue is that some of my overdub tracks don't sync up, theres a slight lag. If that was fixed Id give 5 stars

Appendix 2

Id	Date/time	Rating	Review
18	2014-01-24 T00:27:13Z	5	easy.uncomplicated fab 4 quicky ideas on the wing, i rec 3 acstic gittars/vox no prob . . . slight latency but theres little slider to correct. 9/10 and its free!! :)
19	2014-05-24 T23:19:34Z	5	Crazy useful I love this app—I use it frequently lay down tracks for work in progress. I've even imported the wav files to my mixing software as the starting point. It has made it easy for me to stick to my write a song a day regimen. Thanks!
20	2014-07-25 T00:48:05Z	5	Perfect Omg this is the fastest way to quickly mock up a song! Just sing and play into your phone a few times and my little joke recordings are suddenly a pretty big production! No weird permissions or persistent background processes, this is how android should be.
21	2014-01-03 T05:19:29Z	5	Awesome Had some issues initially, the speedy response from the developer was very helpful and I was able to solve my problems. Everything works great now. Thanks. Extremely useful app.
22	2013-11-02 T23:47:10Z	4	Pretty good, but a little buggy. Unbeatable price (free). Sometimes truncates songs when switching back and forth between landscape and portrait modes. Other than that, a fun and useful thought-catching tool.
23	2013-11-13 T00:39:15Z	1	It doesn't work. After every time I bounce a track, say a guitar part. And I leave the app to, I dunno, read the lyrics to the song I'm recording, It deletes the master. This is ridiculous
24	2014-07-29 T01:52:33Z	5	Jodiah Tip 1 keep screen on, disable sleep modes. Tip 2 disable auto rotate, after that I've had no problems.
25	2014-04-12 T23:27:50Z	4	Me gustó A la hora de reproducir la grabación en la app esta algo desfasado, pero cuando revise lo que grabo . . . :-) me encanta. Sólo deberían hacer un poco más simple aprender a usarlo, de ahí en fuera . . . Me gusta. Mucho

References

Ableton. n.d. "Learn More about Ableton—Maker of Live and Push | Ableton." Accessed June 3, 2019. https://www.ableton.com/en/about/.

Acustica. n.d. "Analog Sampled Plugins for Mixing and Mastering—Acustica Audio." Accessed March 18, 2021. https://www.acustica-audio.com/store/en.

Ajiboye, Tolu. 2017. "Breaking the Code: How Women in Nigeria Are Changing the Face of Tech." *The Guardian*, August 15, 2017. https://www.theguardian.com/lifeandstyle/2017/aug/14/breaking-the-code-how-women-in-nigeria-are-changing-the-face-of-tech.

Allen-Robertson, James. 2017. "The Materiality of Digital Media: The Hard Disk Drive, Phonograph, Magnetic Tape and Optical Media in Technical Close-up." *New Media & Society* 19 (3): 455–70.

Amrani, Iman, and Noah Payne-Frank. 2017. "Run the Code: Is Algorave the Future of Dance Music?" *The Guardian*, November 30 2017. https://www.theguardian.com/music/2017/nov/30/is-algorave-the-future-of-dance-music-sheffield-algomech-festival.

Andersen, Barbara. 2013. "Tricks, Lies, and Mobile Phones: 'Phone Friend' Stories in Papua New Guinea." *Culture, Theory and Critique* 54 (3): 318–34.

Anderson, Tim J. 2014. *Popular Music in a Digital Music Economy: Problems and Practices for an Emerging Service Industry*. Routledge Research in Music 8. New York: Routledge.

Android. n.d. "Build for Billions." Android Developers. Accessed February 18, 2022. https://developer.android.com/docs/quality-guidelines/build-for-billions.

Arditi, David. 2015. *iTake-over: The Recording Industry in the Digital Era*. Lanham, MD: Rowman & Littlefield.

———. 2018. "Digital Subscriptions: The Unending Consumption of Music in the Digital Era." *Popular Music and Society* 41 (3): 302–18.

———. 2019. "Music Everywhere: Setting a Digital Music Trap." *Critical Sociology* 45 (4-5): 617–30.

———. 2021. *Streaming Culture: Subscription Platforms and the Unending Consumption of Culture*. Emerald Group Publishing.

Audio Engineering Society. 2000. "Thomas Stockham III—AES Live: Legends." Accessed Jan 8, 2020. https://aes.digitellinc.com/aes/sessions/1963/view

AudioSet. n.d. "AudioSet." Accessed February 17, 2022. https://research.google.com/audioset//index.html.

Barbour, E. 1998. "The Cool Sound of Tubes [Vacuum Tube Musical Applications]." *Spectrum, IEEE* 35 (8): 24–35.

Bates, Eliot. 2004. "Glitches, Bugs, and Hisses: The Degeneration of Musical Recordings and the Contemporary Musical Work." In *Bad Music: The Music We Love to Hate*, edited by Christopher J. Washburne and Maiken Derno, 275–93. London: Routledge.

———. 2010. "Mixing for Parlak and Bowing for a Büyük Ses: The Aesthetics of Arranged Traditional Music in Turkey." *Ethnomusicology* 54 (1): 81–105.

———. 2016. *Digital Tradition: Arrangement and Labor in Istanbul's Recording Studio Culture*. Oxford University Press.

Bell, Adam, Ethan Hein, and Jarrod Ratcliffe. 2015. "Beyond Skeuomorphism: The Evolution of Music Production Software User Interface Metaphors." *Journal on the Art of Record Production* 9.

Bell, Adam Patrick. 2018. *Dawn of the DAW: The Studio as Musical Instrument*. Oxford University Press.

Bennett, Samantha. 2012. "Endless Analogue: Situating Vintage Technologies in the Contemporary Recording & Production Workplace." *Journal on the Art of Record Production*, no. 7. https://www.arpjournal.com/asarpwp/endless-analogue-situating-vintage-technologies-in-the-contemporary-recording-production-workplace/.

Bergström, Ilias, and Alan F. Blackwell. 2016. "The Practices of Programming." In *2016 IEEE Symposium on Visual Languages and Human-Centric Computing (VL/HCC)*, 190–98.

Berry, D. 2016. *The Philosophy of Software: Code and Mediation in the Digital Age*. Springer.

Berry, Dave M. 2011. "The Computational Turn: Thinking About the Digital Humanities," *Culture Machine* 12.

Bird, S. Elizabeth. 2011. "Are We All Produsers Now?" *Cultural Studies* 25 (4-5): 502–16.

Borschke, Margie. 2017. *This Is Not a Remix: Piracy, Authenticity and Popular Music*. Bloomsbury Publishing USA.

Bosma, Hannah. 2016. "Gender and Technological Failures in Glitch Music." *Contemporary Music Review* 35 (1): 102–14.

Brian, Nicholas J., Jorge Herrera, Jieun Oh, and Ge Wang. 2010. "Momu: A Mobile Music Toolkit." In *Proceedings of the 2010 Conference on New Interfaces for Musical Expression (NIME 2010)*. Sydney, Australia.

Briar. n.d. "Secure Messaging, Anywhere—Briar." Accessed September 19, 2020. https://briarproject.org/.

Brooks, Grace, Amandine Pras, Athena Elafros, and Monica Lockett. 2021. "Do We Really Want to Keep the Gate Threshold That High?" *Journal of the Audio Engineering Society* 69 (4): 238–60.

Brøvig-Hanssen, Ragnhild, and Anne Danielsen. 2016. *Digital Signatures: The Impact of Digitization on Popular Music Sound / Ragnhild Brøvig-Hanssen and Anne Danielsen.* Cambridge, MA: The MIT Press.

Brunton, Finn. 2018. "Wechat: Messaging Apps and New Social Currency Transaction Tools." In *Appified: Culture in the Age of Apps / Jeremy Wade Morris and Sarah Murray, Editors*, edited by Jeremy Wade Morris and Sarah Murray, 179–87. Ann Arbor: University of Michigan Press.

Carreras, Ricardo, and Alaganandan Ganeshkumar. 2018. Audio Device with Wakeup Word Detection. US20180366117A1, issued December 2018.

Cascone, Kim. 2000. "The Aesthetics of Failure: "Post-Digital" Tendencies in Contemporary Computer Music." *Computer Music Journal* 24 (4): 12–18.

Ceruzzi, Paul. 2013. "The Historical Context." In *The SAGE Handbook of Digital Technology Research*, 9–25. London: SAGE Publications Ltd.

Chadabe, Joel. 1997. *Electric Sound: The Past and Promise of Electronic Music.* Upper Saddle River, NJ: Prentice Hall.

Cheung, May. 2019. "Reflections on Learning Live Coding as a Musician." In *Proceedings of the Fourth International Conference on Live Coding*, 8. Medialab Prado, Madrid.

Chromium. n.d. "Source/Platform/Audio—Chromium/Blink—Git at Google." Accessed February 16, 2022. https://chromium.googlesource.com/chromium/blink/+/master/Source/platform/audio/.

Chuck. n.d. "ChucK—[Language Specification: Time]." Accessed February 17, 2022. https://chuck.cs.princeton.edu/doc/language/time.html#now.

Chun, Wendy Hui Kyong. 2011. *Programmed Visions: Software and Memory.* Cambridge, MA: MIT Press.

Coleman, E. Gabriella. 2013. *Coding Freedom: The Ethics and Aesthetics of Hacking.* Princeton University Press.

Collins, Karen. 2013. *Playing with Sound: A Theory of Interacting with Sound and Music in Video Games.* Cambridge, MA: MIT Press.

Collins, Nick. 2007. "Musical Robots and Listening Machines." In *The Cambridge Companion to Electronic Music*, edited by Nick Collins and Julio d'Escrivan, 1st ed., 171–200. Cambridge University Press.

———. 2017. "Corposing a History of Electronic Music." *Leonardo Music Journal* 27 (September): 47–48.

Collins, Nick, and Julio d' Escrivan Rincón. 2007. *The Cambridge Companion to Electronic Music.* Cambridge Companions to Music. Cambridge: Cambridge University Press.

Crawford, Kate. 2016. "Artificial Intelligence's White Guy Problem—the New York Times." *New York Times,* June 25, 2016.

Crowdy, Denis. 2007. "Studios at Home in the Solomon Islands: A Case Study of Homesound Studios, Honiara." *The World of Music* 49 (1): 143–54.

———. 2015. "When Digital Is Physical and Ethnomusicologists Are File Sharers." *Journal of World Popular Music* 2 (1): 61–77.

———. 2016. *Hearing the Future: The Music and Magic of the Sanguma Band*. Music and Performing Arts of Asia and the Pacific. Honolulu: University of Hawai'i Press.

Csound. n.d. "Get Started | Csound Community." Accessed February 18, 2022. https://csound.com/get-started.html.

Csound. n.d.b "Home | Csound Community." Accessed February 18, 2022. https://csound.com/.

Dahl, Luke, and Ge Wang. 2010. "Sound Bounce: Physical Metaphors in Designing Mobile Music Performance." In *NIME*, 178–81.

Daniel, Ryan. 2019. "Digital Disruption in the Music Industry: The Case of the Compact Disc." *Creative Industries Journal* 12 (2): 159–66.

D'Errico, Michael Anthony. 2016. "Interface Aesthetics: Sound, Software, and the Ecology of Digital Audio Production." Ph.D., University of California, Los Angeles.

Diettrich, Brian. 2016. "Virtual Micronesia: Performance and Participation in a Pacific Facebook Community." *Perfect Beat* 17 (1): 52–70.

Dijck, José van. 2018. *The Platform Society: Public Values in a Connective World / José van Dijck, Thomas Poell, and Martijn de Waal*. New York: Oxford University Press.

Dixon, Simon, Emilia Gómez, and Anja Volk. 2018. "Editorial: Introducing the Transactions of the International Society for Music Information Retrieval." *Transactions of the International Society for Music Information Retrieval* 1 (1): 1–3.

Doornbusch, Paul. 2004. "Computer Sound Synthesis in 1951: The Music of CSIRAC." *Computer Music Journal* 28 (1): 10–25.

———. 2018. "www.doornbusch.net." Accessed Aug 27, 2018. "http://www.doornbusch.net/CSIRAC/"

Ensmenger, Nathan L. 2003. "Letting the 'Computer Boys' Take over: Technology and the Politics of Organizational Transformation." *International Review of Social History* 48 (S11): 153–80.

———. 2010. *The Computer Boys Take over: Computers, Programmers, and the Politics of Technical Expertise*. Cambridge, MA: MIT Press.

Finn, Ed. 2017. *What Algorithms Want: Imagination in the Age of Computing / Ed Finn*. Book Collections on Project MUSE. Cambridge, MA: MIT Press.

Fuchsia. n.d. "Fuchsia." Accessed February 18, 2022. https://fuchsia.dev/.

Gareus, Robin. 2017. "The Ardour DAW—Latency Compensation and Anywhere-to-Anywhere Signal Routing Systems." PhD Thesis, Paris: Université Paris VIII.

Gay, Leslie C. 1998. "Acting up, Talking Tech: New York Rock Musicians and Their Metaphors of Technology." *Ethnomusicology* 42 (1): 81–98.

Gaye, Lalya, Lars Erik Holmquist, Frauke Behrendt, and Atau Tanaka. 2006. "Mobile Music Technology: Report on an Emerging Community." In *Proceedings of the 2006 Conference on New Interfaces for Musical Expression*, 22–25. IRCAM—Centre Pompidou.

Goggin, Gerard. 2006. *Cell Phone Culture: Mobile Technology in Everyday Life*. London: Routledge.
Goodman, Romello. 2020. "Code Is Sourdough—Increment: Remote." Accessed Nov 24, 2020. https://increment.com/remote/code-is-sourdough/.
Google. n.d. "Billions" Android Developers. Accessed Jan 7, 2020. https://developers.google.com/web/billions/.
Google About. n.d. "Google—About Google, Our Culture & Company News." Accessed July 12, 2020. //www.google.com.au/.
Google Research. n.d. "Google Research." Accessed February 18, 2022. https://research.google/.
Gopinath, Sumanth. 2005. "Ringtones, or the Auditory Logic of Globalization." *First Monday* 10 (12). http://firstmonday.org/ojs/index.php/fm/article/view/1295.
Gopinath, Sumanth S. 2013. *The Ringtone Dialectic: Economy and Cultural Form*. Cambridge, MA: MIT Press.
Greene, Paul D. 2005. "Introduction: Wired Sound and Sonic Cultures." In *Wired for Sound: Engineering and Technologies in Sonic Cultures*, edited by Paul D. Greene and Thomas Porcello, 1–22. Middletown, CT: Wesleyan University Press.
Greene, Paul D., and Thomas Porcello, eds. 2005. *Wired for Sound: Engineering and Technologies in Sonic Cultures*. Middletown, CT: Wesleyan University Press.
Grosse, Darwin. 2018. "Art + Music + Technology: Podcast 214: Paul Davis (Ardour)." Accessed March 17, 2021. https://artmusictech.libsyn.com/podcast-214-paul-davis-ardour.
Guardian Culture. 2017. *Run the Code: Is Algorave the Future of Dance Music?* Accessed July 3, 2021. https://www.youtube.com/watch?v=h340aNznHnM.
Harkins, Paul. 2015. "Following the Instruments, Designers, and Users: The Case of the Fairlight CMI." *Journal on the Art of Record Production*, no. 10.
———. 2019. *Digital Sampling: The Design and Use of Music Technologies*. New York: Routledge.
Harlin, Jesse. 2011. "Let's Do the Time Warp Again—Revisiting the Chiptune." *Game Developer*, January: 56.
Harrison. n.d. "Mixbus—Audio Recording Software—DAW Nashville, TN." Accessed May 5, 2020. https://harrisonconsoles.com/product/mixbus/.
Hayles, N. K. 2004. "Print Is Flat, Code Is Deep: The Importance of Media-Specific Analysis." *Poetics Today* 25 (1): 67–90.
Hesmondhalgh, David, and Leslie M. Meier. 2018. "What the Digitalisation of Music Tells Us About Capitalism, Culture and the Power of the Information Technology Sector." *Information, Communication & Society* 21 (11): 1555–70.
Hexter. n.d. "Hexter." Accessed Feb 16, 2022. https://github.com/smbolton/hexter/blob/1cf1bfea5962f7c9726e0cf809b762b3b2655225/src/dx7_voice.c.
Hofstetter, Fred T. 1981. "Applications of the GUIDO System to Aural Skills Research, 1975–1980." *College Music Symposium* 21 (2): 46–53.
Holzapfel, Andre, Bob L. Sturm, and Mark Coeckelbergh. 2018. "Ethical Dimensions of Music Information Retrieval Technology." *Transactions of the International Society for Music Information Retrieval* 1 (1): 44–55.

Horning, Susan Schmidt. 2004. "Engineering the Performance: Recording Engineers, Tacit Knowledge and the Art of Controlling Sound." *Social Studies of Science* 34 (5): 703–31.

Hughes, Diane, Mark Evans, Guy Morrow, and Sarah Keith. 2016. *The New Music Industries: Disruption and Discovery*. Springer.

Hulaud, Stephane. United States Patent: 9934785—Identification of taste attributes from an audio signal. 9934785, issued April 2018.

Hutchby, Ian. 2001. "Technologies, Texts and Affordances." *Sociology* 35 (2): 441–56.

Kamp, Michiel, Tim Summers, and Mark Sweeney, eds. 2016. *Ludomusicology: Approaches to Video Game Music*. Genre, Music and Sound. Sheffield: Equinox Publishing.

Kealy, Edward R. 1979. "From Craft to Art." *Work and Occupations* 6 (1): 3–29.

Kirschenbaum, Matthew G. 2008. *Mechanisms: New Media and the Forensic Imagination*. Cambridge, MA: MIT Press.

Kitchin, Rob, and Martin Dodge. 2011. *Code/Space: Software and Everyday Life*. Cambridge, MA: MIT Press.

Kobie, Nicole. 2017. "Android Overtakes Windows to Become the Internet's Most Popular OS." *Wired UK*. https://www.wired.co.uk/article/android-overtakes-windows.

Kopf, Dan. 2019. "The Economics of Streaming Is Making Songs Shorter." *Quartz*. https://qz.com/1519823/is-spotify-making-songs-shorter/.

Koutsomichalis, Marinos. 2016. "From Music to Big Music: Listening in the Age of Big Data." *Leonardo Music Journal* 26 (1): 24–27.

Latency Native. n.d. "Becoming Latency-Native." Accessed February 17, 2022. https://latencynative.com/.

Leyshon, Andrew. 2014. *Reformatted: Code, Networks, and the Transformation of the Music Industry*. Oxford University Press.

Libsndfile. n.d. "Libsndfile." Accessed February 16, 2022. http://www.mega-nerd.com/libsndfile/.

Lysloff, René T. A. 1997. "Mozart in Mirrorshades: Ethnomusicology, Technology, and the Politics of Representation." *Ethnomusicology* 41 (2): 206–19.

Lysloff, René T. A., and Leslie C. Gay Jr. 2003. *Music and Technoculture*. Wesleyan University Press.

Mačák, Jaromír. 2012. "Real-Time Digital Simulation of Guitar Amplifiers as Audio Effects." Doctoral thesis, Brno University Of Technology.

Mackenzie, Adrian. 2006. *Cutting Code: Software and Sociality*. Peter Lang.

Magnusson, Thor. 2019. *Sonic Writing: Technologies of Material, Symbolic, and Signal Inscriptions*. New York, NY, USA: Bloomsbury Academic, Bloomsbury Publishing Inc.

———. 2006. "Affordances and Constraints in Screen-Based Musical Instruments." In *Proceedings of the 4th Nordic Conference on Human-Computer Interaction: Changing Roles*, 441–44. NordiCHI '06. Oslo, Norway: Association for Computing Machinery.

Manning, Peter. 2004. *Electronic and Computer Music / Peter Manning*. Rev. and expanded ed. New York: Oxford University Press.

Marino, Mark C. 2020. *Critical Code Studies*. MIT Press.

Meintjes, Louise. 2003. *Sound of Africa!: Making Music Zulu in a South African Studio*. Durham: Duke University Press.

Miller, Kiri. 2009. "Schizophonic Performance: Guitar Hero, Rock Band, and Virtual Virtuosity." *Journal of the Society for American Music* 3 (4): 395–429.

Mineo, Liz. 2017. "When It Comes to Internet Privacy, Be Very Afraid, Analyst Suggests." Accessed August 31, 2017. https://news.harvard.edu/gazette/story/2017/08/when-it-comes-to-internet-privacy-be-very-afraid-analyst-suggests/.

"Mobile Operating System Market Share Worldwide." 2022. StatCounter. Accessed February 18, 2022. https://gs.statcounter.com/os-market-share/mobile/worldwide.

Montfort, N., P. Baudoin, J. Bell, I. Bogost, J. Douglass, M. C. Marino, and M. Mateas. 2014. *10 Print Chr$(205. 5+rnd(1)); : Goto 10*. Cambridge, MA: MIT Press.

Moreau, François. 2013. "The Disruptive Nature of Digitization: The Case of the Recorded Music Industry." *International Journal of Arts Management* 15 (2): 18–31.

Morris, Jeremy Wade. 2015. *Selling Digital Music, Formatting Culture*. University of California Press.

Morris, Jeremy, and Evan Elkins. 2015. "FCJ-181 There's a History for That: Apps and Mundane Software as Commodity." *The Fibreculture Journal*, no. 25 (November): 63–88.

Morris, Jeremy Wade, and Sarah Murray. 2018. *Appified: Culture in the Age of Apps / Jeremy Wade Morris and Sarah Murray, Editors*. Ann Arbor: University of Michigan Press.

Mosco, Vincent. 2005. *The Digital Sublime: Myth, Power, and Cyberspace*. University Press Group Limited.

Mozilla. n.d. "Web Audio API—Web APIs | MDN." Accessed February 16, 2022. https://developer.mozilla.org/en-US/docs/Web/API/Web_Audio_API.

MusicKit. 2009. "The MusicKit—Documentation." Accessed February 16, 2022. https://sourceforge.net/projects/musickit/files/MK/5.6.2/.

Nag, Wenche. 2018. "Music Streams, Smartphones, and the Self." *Mobile Media & Communication* 6 (1): 19–36.

Nakamura, Lisa. 2002. *Cybertypes: Race, Ethnicity, and Identity on the Internet*. New York: Routledge.

NAMM. n.d. "Peter Vogel." Accessed February 16, 2022. https://www.namm.org/library/oral-history/peter-vogel.

Nilson, Click. 2007. "Live Coding Practice." In *Proceedings of the 7th International Conference on New Interfaces for Musical Expression*, 112–17. NIME '07. New York, New York: Association for Computing Machinery.

Nordgård, Daniel. 2018. *The Music Business and Digital Impacts: Innovations and Disruptions in the Music Industries*. Springer.

O'Grady, Pat. 2018. "Latent Elements in Pop Music Production." *Popular Music and Society* 41 (5): 506–21.

———. 2019. "The Politics of Digitizing Analogue Recording Technologies." In *Producing Music*, edited by Russ Hepworth-Sawyer, Jay Hodgson, and Mark Marrington, 119–133. Routledge.

Oh, Jieun, Jorge Herrera, Nicholas J. Brian, Luke Dahl, and Ge Wang. 2010. "Evolving the Mobile Phone Orchestra." In *Proceedings of the 2010 Conference on New Interfaces for Musical Expression (NIME 2010)*. Sydney, Australia.

Oliver, Julian. 2006. "The Game Is Not the Medium." http://ljudmila.org/~julian/share/text/The-Game-is-not-the-Medium_Oliver-2006.pdf.

Padios, Jan Maginhay. 2014. "Can You Hear Us Now? Ringtones and Politics in the Contemporary Philippines." In *The Oxford Handbook of Mobile Music Studies Volume 1*, edited by Sumanth Gopinath and Jason Stanyek, 359–81. Oxford University Press.

Pakarinen, Jyri, and David T Yeh. 2009. "A Review of Digital Techniques for Modeling Vacuum-Tube Guitar Amplifiers." *Computer Music Journal* 33 (June): 85–100.

Paul, Leonard J. 2014. "For the Love of Chiptune." In *The Oxford Handbook of Interactive Audio*, edited by Karen Collins, Bill Kapralos, and Holly Tessler, 507–30. Oxford University Press.

Perlman, Marc. 2003. "Consuming Audio: An Introduction to Tweak Theory." In *Music and Technoculture*, edited by Rene Lysloff and Leslie Gay, 346–57. Middletown, CT: Wesleyan University Press.

Perlroth, Nicole. 2019. "Apple Was Slow to Act on FaceTime Bug That Allows Spying on IPhones." *The New York Times*, January 30, 2019, sec. Technology. https://www.nytimes.com/2019/01/29/technology/facetime-glitch-apple.html.

Petersen, George. 2010. "In Memoriam-Keith Barr 1949-2010." August 25, 2010. https://web.archive.org/web/20100829053857/http://mixonline.com/news/keith_barr_obit_2508/index1.html.

Piatier, Andre. 1988. "Transectorial Innovations and the Transformation of Firms." *The Information Society* 5 (4): 205–31.

Pierce, David. 2017. "Steve Lacy Produced That Hot Kendrick Lamar Track Using Only His iPhone." *Wired*. April 14, 2017. https://www.wired.com/2017/04/steve-lacy-iphone-producer/.

Porcello, Thomas. 2004. "Speaking of Sound: Language and the Professionalization of Sound-Recording Engineers." *Social Studies of Science* 34 (5): 733–58.

Prior, Nick. 2008. "Putting a Glitch in the Field: Bourdieu, Actor Network Theory and Contemporary Music." *Cultural Sociology* 2 (3): 301–19.

Randolph, Robert. 2018. "Interview with Paul Davis of Ardour about Ardour 6.0 and More." Accessed February 17, 2022. https://www.admiralbumblebee.com/music/2018/02/20/Interview-with-Paul-Davis-of-Ardour-about-Ardour-6-and-more.html.

Razlogiva, Elena. 2018. "Shazam: The Blind Spots of Algorithmic Music Recognition and Recommendation." In *Appified: Culture in the Age of Apps*, edited by Jeremy Wade Morris and Sarah Murray, 257–66. Ann Arbor: University of Michigan Press.

Redhead, Tracy. 2015. "Composing and Recording for Fluid Digital Music Forms." *Journal on the Art of Record Production* 10.

Reid, George. 2018. "Chiptune: The Ludomusical Shaping of Identity." *The Computer Games Journal* 7 (4): 279–90.
Renzo, Adrian, and Steve Collins. 2017. "Technologically Mediated Transparency in Music Production." *Popular Music and Society* 40 (4): 406–21.
Rosenberg, Scott. 2008. *Dreaming in Code: Two Dozen Programmers, Three Years, 4,732 Bugs, and One Quest for Transcendent Software*. Crown Business.
Rowe, Robert. 1992. "Machine Listening and Composing with Cypher." *Computer Music Journal* 16 (1): 43–63.
Sangild, Torben. 2004. "Glitch—the Beauty of Malfunction." In *Bad Music: The Music We Love to Hate*, edited by Christopher J. Washburne and Maiken Derno, 257–74. London: Routledge.
Schmitz, Thomas, and Jean J. Embrechts. 2013. "Nonlinear Guitar Loudspeaker Simulation." In *Audio Engineering Society Convention 134*.
Shepherd, Tamara, and Christopher Cwynar. 2018. "Yik Yak: From Anonymity to Identification." In *Appified: Culture in the Age of Apps / Jeremy Wade Morris and Sarah Murray, Editors*, edited by Jeremy Wade Morris and Sarah Murray, 169–78. Ann Arbor: University of Michigan Press.
Smajstrla, Ann. 2020. "Epic Games CEO Speaks out against Apple, Google App Store 'Monopoly.'" Accessed Aug 4, 2020. https://au.news.yahoo.com/fortnite-developer-ceo-against-apple-google-monopoly-app-stores-212648207.html.
Sony. n.d. "Sony Group Portal—Sony History Chapter 7 Making Digital Audio a Reality." Accessed February 16, 2022. https://www.sony.com/en/SonyInfo/CorporateInfo/History/SonyHistory/2-07.html.
South, Oscar. 2019. "Thoughts on Live Coding as a Session Musician (1 of 3)—TOPLAP." Accessed Feb 1, 2021. https://toplap.org/thoughts-on-live-coding-as-a-session-musician-1-of-3/.
———. 2019b. "Thoughts On Live Coding As A Session Musician (2 of 3)—TOPLAP." Accessed February 1, 2021. https://toplap.org/thoughts-on-live-coding-as-a-session-musician-2-of-3/.
Spice, Byron. 2015. "Questioning the Fairness of Targeting Ads Online." Accessed August 22, 2017. https://www.cmu.edu/news/stories/archives/2015/july/online-ads-research.html.
Spotify. 2019. "Privacy Policy." Accessed Nov 4, 2019. https://www.spotify.com/au/legal/privacy-policy/#s4.
Sterne, Jonathan. 2006. "What's Digital in Digital Music?" In *Digital Media: Transformations in Human Communication*, edited by Paul Messaris and Lee Humphreys, 95–109. Peter Lang.
———. 2012. *Mp3: The Meaning of a Format*. Durham, NC: Duke University Press.
———. 2014a. "There Is No Music Industry." *Media Industries* 1 (1).
———. 2014b. "A Manifesto For Music Technologists." Accessed May 26, 2014. http://www.musictechifesto.org/.
Strachan, Robert. 2017. *Sonic Technologies: Popular Music, Digital Culture and the Creative Process*. United States: Bloomsbury Publishing.

Stuart, Caleb. 2003. "Damaged Sound: Glitching and Skipping Compact Discs in the Audio of Yasunao Tone, Nicolas Collins and Oval." *Leonardo Music Journal* 13: 47–52.

Superpowered. 2016. "Android Audio's 10 Millisecond Problem: The Android Audio Path Latency Explainer." Accessed August 25, 2016. https://superpowered.com/androidaudiopathlatency.

Tanaka, Atau. 2004. "Mobile Music Making." In *Proceedings of the 2004 Conference on New Interfaces for Musical Expression*, 154–56. National University of Singapore.

———. 2014. "Creative Applications of Interactive Mobile Music." In *The Oxford Handbook of Mobile Music Studies, Volume 2*, edited by Sumanth Gopinath and Jason Stanyek, 2:470–86. New York: Oxford University Press.

Taylor, Timothy D. 2012. *The Sounds of Capitalism: Advertising, Music, and the Conquest of Culture*. University of Chicago Press.

Telban, Borut, and Daniela Vávrová. 2014. "Ringing the Living and the Dead: Mobile Phones in a Sepik Society." *The Australian Journal of Anthropology* 25 (2): 223–38.

Théberge, Paul. 1997. *Any Sound You Can Imagine: Making Music/Consuming Technology*. Wesleyan University Press.

ToneJs. 2017. "Feature Request: Choke Groups for MultiPlayer · Issue #252 · Tonejs/Tone.Js." Accessed Nov 11, 2020. https://github.com/Tonejs/Tone.js/issues/252.

———. n.d. "TransportTime · Tonejs/Tone.Js Wiki." GitHub. Accessed February 18, 2022. https://github.com/Tonejs/Tone.js.

Tiku, Nitasha. 2017. "That Google 'Anti-Diversity' Memo Really Put Executives in a Bind | WIRED." *Wired*. August 7, 2017. https://www.wired.com/story/google-manifesto-puts-executives-in-a-bind/.

Turino, Thomas. 2009. "Four Fields of Music Making and Sustainable Living." *The World of Music* 51 (1): 95–117.

Ullman, Ellen. 1997. *Close to the Machine: Technophilia and Its Discontents: A Memoir / by Ellen Ullman*. San Francisco: City Lights Books.

Vaarzon-Morel, Petronella. 2014. "Pointing the Phone: Transforming Technologies and Social Relations Among Warlpiri." *The Australian Journal of Anthropology* 25 (2): 239–55.

Volz, Dustin, and Supantha Mukherjee. 2016. "Twitter Cuts Jobs with Eye on 2017 Profit; Vine Discontinued." *Reuters*, October 27, 2016. https://www.reuters.com/article/us-twitter-results-idUSKCN12R1GW.

W3C. n.d. "About W3C." Accessed February 16, 2022. https://www.w3.org/Consortium/.

Wang, Ge. 2014. "The World Is Your Stage: Making Music on the iPhone." In *The Oxford Handbook of Mobile Music Studies, Volume 2*, edited by Sumanth Gopinath and Jason Stanyek, 2:487–504. New York: Oxford University Press.

———. 2007. "A History of Programming and Music." In *The Cambridge Companion to Electronic Music*, edited by Nick Collins and Julio d'Escrivan, 1st ed., 55–86. Cambridge University Press.

———. 2018. *Artful Design: Technology in Search of the Sublime, a Musicomic Manifesto*. Stanford University Press.

Wang, Ge, Perry R. Cook, and Spencer Salazar. 2015. "ChucK: A Strongly Timed Computer Music Language." *Computer Music Journal* 39 (4): 10–29.

Wang, Ge, Georg Essl, and Henri Penttinen. 2014. "The Mobile Phone Orchestra." In *The Oxford Handbook of Mobile Music Studies, Volume 2*, edited by Sumanth Gopinath and Jason Stanyek, 453–69. New York: Oxford University Press.

Wang, Ge, Georg Essl, Jeff Smith, Spencer Salazar, P. Cook, Rob Hamilton, Rebecca Fiebrink, et al. 2009. "Smule= Sonic Media: An Intersection of the Mobile, Musical, and Social." In *Proceedings of the International Computer Music Conference*, 283–86.

Wang, Ge, Spencer Salazar, Jieun Oh, and Robert Hamilton. 2015. "World Stage: Crowdsourcing Paradigm for Expressive Social Mobile Music." *Journal of New Music Research* 44 (2): 112–28.

Warren, Tom, and Jacob Kastrenakes. 2019. "Apple Blocks Facebook from Running Its Internal IOS Apps—The Verge." Accessed April 15, 2019. https://www.theverge.com/2019/1/30/18203551/apple-facebook-blocked-internal-ios-apps.

WebAudio. n.d. "Webaudio—Mozsearch." Accessed February 16, 2022. https://searchfox.org/mozilla-central/source/dom/media/webaudio.

WebAudio. 2013. "Web Audio Processing: Use Cases and Requirements." Accessed March 16, 2021. https://www.w3.org/TR/webaudio-usecases/#acknowledgements.

———. 2021a. "Web Audio API." Accessed February 16, 2022. https://www.w3.org/TR/webaudio/#introductory.

———. 2021b. "Web Audio API." Accessed February 18, 2022. https://www.w3.org/TR/webaudio/#audio-glitching.

Wikström, Patrik, and Robert DeFillippi. 2016. *Business Innovation and Disruption in the Music Industry*. Edward Elgar Publishing.

Williamson, John, and Martin Cloonan. 2007. "Rethinking the Music Industry." *Popular Music* 26 (2): 305–22.

Index

Ableton, 68, 70
Acustica audio, 59
ADAT, 26, 29–30
aesthetics, 8, 56–59
affordances, 17, 35, 45
Africa, 96, 99
algorave, 63
algorithms, 34
Allen–Robertson, James, 15
amplifiers, 57, 58
analog: computers, 22n1; consoles, 27; filter circuit, 37, 217; instruments, 8; knowledge translation, 30, 31; non–linearity, 58; signal, 12; vintage gear, 27
Android. See operating system
appification. See apps
Apple, 27, 32, 99; app store, 83; devices, 19; Facetime bug 2; iOS. See operating system
application programming interface (API), 46, 48, 51
apps, 1, 72, 74–75, 80, 84; appification, 67, 82, 99, 107; centralization, 84, 90; data collection, 74, 84; developer portal, 73–74; developer/user connection, 75; development of, 80, 81; distribution of, 73–74, 79, 83–84, 90; economics of, 75, 83, 84, 90; rating and reviews, 74–78; Twotrack, 6, 8
archiving, 111
Arditi, David, 1, 4, 88
Ardour. See Digital Audio Workstation
audio engineers, 34n2

Bates, Eliot, 55, 67, 102
Bell, Adam, 16, 37
Bennett, Samantha, 27
Berry, Dave, 46
big music, 96
Bird, S. Elizabeth, 91
Bluetooth, 1
Bosma, Hannah, 55
Brooks, Grace, 34
Brøvig–Hanssen, Ragnhild, 21
Brunton, 83
bugs, 17

capitalism, 96
Cascone, Kim, 54
CCRMA, 43
CD, 12–13, 15, 18, 54, 107
CD, experimental use, 56
cell phones, 8, 97–98
Chadabe, Joel, 27
Cheung, May, 64
China, 99

ChucK, 40–42
Chun, Wendy, 103–4
CNMAT, 43
code: abstractions, 47; agency of, 4; as cultural heritage, 110; assembly, 17; closed source, 18; execution, 17; layers, 21; library, 46, 50–51; library, layers, 47; lifecycle, 18; nature of, 18; obscurity of, 6; one liner, 20; ontology, 11, 20; and space/s, 101–2; structure of, 17; unintended sonic consequences, 56;
codebase, 69
codejects, 19, 87, 115
coding: and diversity, 33–34; as musicianship, 66; and values, 102
Coleman, E. Gabriella, 68
Collins, Karen, 62
Collins, Steve, 67
commerce, advertising, 106
Commodore 64, 20
computer games, 110
computer languages, 8, 17. See also programming language
computer program, 17
computers: early personal, 25; history, 23–24
constraints, 15, 17, 35
conversion, digital to analog, 1
copyright, royalty income, 99
CPU, 17
critical code studies, 6
Csound, 44, 110
cultural studies, 6, 9
culture, 9

Danielsen, Anne, 21
data: analysis, 95; collection, 6, 89–90, 95; copying, cloning, 18; extraction, 93; format, 12; fragmentation, 13; idea of movement, 87; sequential storage, 14
Davis, Paul, 38, 70
DAW. See Digital Audio Workstation (DAW)

de Castro Lopo, Erik, 46
Demoscene, 63
D'Errico, Michael, 16, 35
design, 57
Dickins, Glenn, 39, 94
Diettrich, Brian, 111
digital: definition of, 4; terminology, 1; digital audio, 38
Digital Audio Workstation (DAW), 27–28, 30, 37, 67; Ardour, 38, 60, 70–71; Bitwig, 102; browser based, 50; development of, 70–71; examples of, 68
digital ethnography, 90
digital humanities, 3–4
digital to analog conversion (DAC), 37, 44
digitalization, 4, 11
digitization, 4, 7, 11–12, 24
disruption, 4
diversity, 9, 68, 82
DJ, 21
Dodge, Martin, 6–7, 17, 19, 101
Dolby, 94

effects, 57
Elkins, Evan, 34, 107
emulation, 16, 53, 59; of analog technology, 15; computer games, 62; digital, 57; as maintaining tradition, 61; trademark conflicts, 61; tubes, 61
engineer: audio, 29, 30; electronic skills, 29; software, 18
Ensmenger, Nathan, 33
Epic Games, 83
ethnomusicology, 6, 67
expertise: computer, 29, 30, 33; music production, 29

Facebook, 32, 95–96, 111
Fairlight CMI, 25, 60
file sharing, 88
form, 104–5

Games, 8–bit sound, 57

Games, Sopwith, 62
gender and diversity, 9, 47, 55, 68
git, 69, 71
glitch, 15, 54; gender politics, 55; as unwanted noise, 55;
Global North, 8, 80
Global South, 9, 79, 96, 106; appification, 99; data collection ethics, 114; dominance of Android, 90, 109; Internet access, 81; mobile computing, 8; software development, 81–82; technology histories, 97
Goggin, Gerard, 97
Google, 3, 32, 48, 83, 111; advertising, 72, 95; corporate mission, 112; data and privacy, 108; developing for Global South, 80–82; Google Play developer console, 75–76, 79, 81; Google Play Store, 84; machine listening, 94, 96; Play store, 6, 72, 81
grammatology, hard drive, 14
Greene, Paul, 3, 35–36
Grosse, Darwin, 70
Guitarix, 58

hard drive, 12
Harrison, 59, 60, 70
Hayles, N.K., 16
Hesmondhalgh, David, 11
history, code and software, 16
Horst, Heather, 80
Hutchby, Ian, 35

industry transformation, 31–32
integrated development environment (IDE), 81
interface, 3–4, 21, 35–36, 46; aesthetics, 16; construction of, 16; gender assumptions, 47
Internet browser, 48–52
iPad, 60, 92
iPhone, 91–92
IRCAM, 43
iTunes, 19

Kincaid, Bill, 19
Kirschenbaum, Matthew, 14, 56
Kitchin, Rob, 6–7, 17, 19, 101
Koutsomichalis, Marinos, 1, 88

Lacy, Steven, 92
LANDR, 92
latency, 36–38, 73, 92, 105
LeBoeuf, Jay, 95. See also Real Industry
libsndfile (library), 46
Linux, 34, 58, 70
listening, 93, 94, 108
live coding, 45, 63–64, 66,

machine listening. See listening
Mackenzie, Adrian, 17, 20
Magnusson, Thor, 2, 16, 23, 35
Marino, Mark, 6
materiality: forensic, 14–15; formal, 14–15
Mathews, Max, 24, 43
Max/MSP, 43
media, 13
media studies, 6
Meier, Leslie M, 11
Meintjes, Louise, 67
Micronesia, 111
MIDI, 26–27
minimum viable product (MVP), 82
MIR, 66
modulation, 101–2
Montfort, N., 23
Morris, Jeremy Wade, 32, 34, 107
Mosco, Vincent, 91
mp3, 5, 13
Murray, Sarah, 82
music commerce, 107; big music, 88; data collection, 92; internet based advertising, 52; platforms, 89; sectorial transformation, 108, 114; service oriented, 32
Music Information Retrieval (MIR), 93, 96
music production, 29, 31

music software, 16, 27, 29, 34, 70, 72; Anglophone bias, 35–36; as cultural heritage, 110; diversity, 68, 82
music streaming, 32
MusicKit, 47
musical time, 13, 36–37, 104; digital representation, 42; notion of "now", 40–41; representation by a DAW, 37–38

Nakamura, Lisa, 47
NeXT, 26
Nicolai, Carsten, 42
Nilson, Click, 64
noise, 13, 55
non–linearity, 58

O'Grady, Pat, 59, 67
One Laptop Per Child (OLPC), 43
Open Sound Control (OSC), 45
open source, 69–71, 111, 115
operating system: Android, 3, 38–40, 72–73, 75, 77, 79–81, 90, 98, 109; Fuchsia, 109; iOS, 39, 79–80, 83–84, 90, 109; Linux, 6, 34, 58, 62, 70–71, 109; MacOS, 26; Windows, 26, 90
orchestra: cellphone, 91; laptop, 91
Oval (artist), 56

Papua New Guinea, 8, 68, 80–81, 97–99
patents, 108
photography, 104
popular music studies, 6, 11
Porcello, Thomas, 3
Prior, Nick, 55
privacy, 2, 108–9
programming language: abstraction of instruments and score, 43; Assembly, 68; C++, 46, 48, 68; Haskell, 45; Java, 20, 46, 109; Javascript, 48, 51; for music, 43; representation of time, 42
ProTools, 71
Puckette, Miller, 68
PureData, 43

racism, 34
Radio, 95–96
Razlogiva, Elena, 82, 93, 96
Real Industry, 31, 95
realtime, 38, 45, 53, 58, 103
Recording studios, equipment, 26
Redhead, Tracy, 21
Renzo, Adrian, 67
Robillard, David, 70
Rosenberg, Scott, 6

Sangild, Torben, 55
Schafer, R. Murray, 104
schizophonia, 104
Schneier, Bruce, 33, 108
search engine optimisation (SEO), 75
sexism, 34
Shazam, 83, 93, 96
signal flow, 1
skeuomorphs, 17, 36
smartphones, 87, 89–90, 97, 108
software: copy protection, 18; definition of, 7; faults in, 2; license, 6; lifecycle, 7, 19; open source, 6; permissions, 6; proprietary, 6; systems and complexity, 19
Software industry, diversity of, 68
Solid State Logic (SSL), 59
Sony, 25, 32
source code, 6, 25, 47–48, 52, 58, 60, 62, 110–11
South, Oscar, 65–66
Spotify, 5, 84, 108–9
SSD, 13–14
Sterne, Jonathan, 89, 112–14
Stockham, Thomas, 24
Strachan, Robert, 16, 21, 35, 37
SuperCollider, 45, 63
Superpowered, 39–40
surveillance, 33
synthesizers, 26
synthesizers, Yamaha DX–7, 60

tape, 13
Taylor, Tim, 95–96

technoculture, 3
time 103. See also musical time
ToneJs (library), 50–51
Tubes (vacuum), 24
Turino, Thomas, 64–65
Twotrack, 8, 72, 82; design, 73; distribution of, 72

UAD, 59
Ullman, Ellen, 18–19

values, musical, 15
Vercoe, Barry, 44
Version control, 51, 69, 71

vinyl, 13
Vogel, Peter, 60

W3C, 48–49, 115
Wang, Ge, 38, 41–42, 57
Web Audio, 48, 110, 112; motivation for development, 52; use cases, 49–50
West Papua, 80
WhatsApp, 32
Wilson, Rebekah, 105

YouTube, 32, 111

About the Author

Denis Crowdy teaches music at Macquarie University in Sydney, Australia. His research explores music technology, music and cell phones, and music in Papua New Guinea. He is an active developer of music and music related software and plays guitar and bass in a number of groups around Sydney.

www.ingramcontent.com/pod-product-compliance
Lightning Source LLC
Chambersburg PA
CBHW020126010526
44115CB00008B/991